# SECRET FRENCH RIVIERA

Jean-Pierre Cassely

Jonglez

# SECRET FRENCH RIVIERA

Jean-Pierre Cassely

*Secret French Riviera* is the result of an observation: the guidebooks available to the inhabitants of French riviera and frequent visitors to the region all seem to describe the same familiar places. There is nothing or very little in them that would surprise anyone who already knows the region fairly well.

This guide is aimed at such readers, although we hope it will also please the occasional visitor seeking to depart from the beaten tourist paths.

Comments about this guidebook and its contents, as well as information concerning places we may not have mentioned herein, are more than welcome. They will permit us to enrich future editions of this guidebook.

Don't hesitate to write us:
• By e-mail: info@editionsjonglez.com
• By post: Éditions Jonglez, 17, boulevard du Roi, 78000 Versailles, France.

# CONTENTS

## MONACO, MENTON AND SURROUNDINGS

## NICE

# AROUND NICE

# CONTENTS

## CANNES, ANTIBES, SAINT-PAUL-DE-VENCE AND SURROUNDINGS

## FRÉJUS, SAINT-RAPHAËL AND SURROUNDINGS

## IN AND AROUND SAINT-TROPEZ

# CONTENTS

## IN AND AROUND DRAGUIGNAN

## IN AND AROUND HYÈRES

**INDEX**

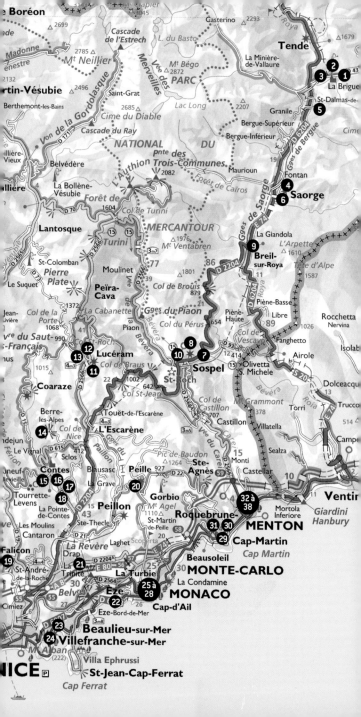

# MONACO, MENTON AND SURROUNDINGS

# THE FRESCOES OF NOTRE-DAME-DES-FONTAINES ❶

RD143, 06430 La Brigue • Opening hours: beware of the times given in guides
because these change (the chapel needs constant surveillance, not always
easy to organize). It's essential to check with the tourist office in La Brigue,
place Saint-Martin • Tel: 04 93 79 09 34

**P**ainted from floor to ceiling, Notre-Dame-des-Fontaines offers one of those rare artistic experiences that have no equal. Some visitors will be reminded of the Scrovegni chapel in Padua where the air is filtered and you have to wait 15 minutes in an airlock. There are no airlocks here but no lighting either. Flash photography is banned and you need a good light outside to properly appreciate these incredible frescoes that are surprisingly well preserved.

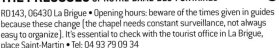

> *Spectacular frescoes with Judas, torso ripped open*

The chapel murals were painted between 1491 and 1492 by the two most prestigious artists of their age: Giovanni Baleison and Giovanni Canavesio. Both Piedmontese but very different characters, they shared the work according to the themes to be treated: sweetness and light for Baleison and severity and shadow for Canavesio. Although several other religious buildings painted between 1450 and 1495 bear their signature, such as the chapelle Saint-Sébastien at Saint-Étienne-de-Tinée, Notre-Dame-des-Fontaines is considered to be their masterwork.

Canavesio's Judas is the most terrifying image among these most unusual frescoes: he is shown hanging, mouth open and tongue lolling. His torso is ripped open and clearly shows his viscera, liver and heart. To the side, a winged demon extracts a homunculus* from the apostle's body. According to St Matthew's Gospel, Judas, after embracing Christ to point Him out to those come to arrest Him, went to the temple to throw back the pieces of silver gained through his treachery and then hang himself.

This chapel is named for the proximity of seven intermittent and miraculous springs.

(*) Homunculus or homuncule: miniature human or humanoid creature.

## SIGHTS NEARBY

### LIME KILN ❷
RD43, 06430 La Brigue

Located on private property, a monumental lime kiln, partly ruined, is a reminder that this border region never stopped building fortifications against the threats from its French neighbours. At the time, defensive works and the existence of road links required the production of lime (the cement of the time, used in most structures) on this site.

Dating from the end of the 19th century, lime was manufactured in this kiln by heating to 1,000 degrees the limestone quarried locally. At the end of the cycle, around 56% of the burned mass was transformed into quicklime and, when it had cooled down, into lime for building purposes.

## THE BEE HOUSE

Quartier de l'Évêché, 06430 La Brigue

*Protecting bees from bears*

A drystone enclosure intended to shelter beehives, the bee houses protect not only the hives, but the bees and their honey from raids by brown bears. Built by the residents of La Brigue from the 16th century onwards, there are still some fifty remaining today. One of these is particularly noticeable beside Notre-Dame-des-Fontaines chapel (route marked Vallée de Bens). Not far from here, the bee house of quartier de l'Évêché would seem to date from 1612 if we are to believe the engraved stone near the entrance door. These *ca d'arbinee*, as the Brigasques call them, were constructed on hillsides, facing the rising sun and near a water source. Such a "house" could hold about 100 hives, known as *bruscs*.

### SIGHTS NEARBY

#### THE STONE OF THE PILLORY
Place de l'Église 06540 Saorge

Above the magnificent village of Saorge, to the left of the church façade, a bluish stone a little bigger than a football could easily go unnoticed. The base of the former village pillory, this stone according to oral tradition dates from the Middle Ages. The pillory or stocks, intended to expose delinquents to public persecution, most often merchants cheating on the quality or quantity of their goods, was only abolished in France in 1848. Tied hand and foot, the culprit had to suffer the gibes, insults, spittle and whatever other pleasantries the crowd came up with. The expression "stock-still" clearly comes from this medieval custom, where the culprit was physically unable to move and escape his fate.

#### THE MUSSOLINIAN STATION OF SAINT-DALMAS-DE-TENDEE

Travellers arriving for the first time at Saint-Dalmas-de-Tende might well ask themselves if there has been no mistake: totally out of proportion to the size of the little town, the station is in fact an immense edifice in the so-called "Mussolinian" style, dating from 1928. Near the border on the Nice–Cuneo line, Saint-Dalmas-de-Tende marked the arrival on Italian territory. The station is now closed and abandoned, even though trains still pass in front of it.

#### PLAQUE COMMEMORATING CONSTRUCTION OF THE NICE–TURIN ROAD
RN204 06540 Saorge

Between two tunnels, on the left bank of the Roia River, an inscription carved in the rock commemorates the completion of the strategic Nice–Turin road, built on the orders of Charles-Emmanuel I of Savoy at the end of the 16th century.

# RESTAURANT ORIENT-EXPRESS

**7**

Gare de Sospel, 06380 Sospel
- Tel. : 06 10 50 61 77
- Tel: 06 10 50 61 77
- Open daily, lunchtime and evening
- Closed Wednesday and Saturday lunchtime
- Set menus €22.50 and €29.50

*A restaurant in a train*

Run by a non-profit-making organization, the Orient-Express restaurant is located in a railway carriage of the former Sud Express line linking Paris with Lisbon via Madrid. Dating from 1938, the carriage was acquired in 1978 at Irun (on the French/Spanish border) from the Compagnie des Wagons-Lits who were gradually selling off their rolling stock as their prestigious lines were cut back because of competition from airlines.

All the restaurant profits being used towards restoring the former railway carriages, we can only invite you to defend this noble cause. The air-conditioned room can seat forty-eight and plunges diners into a luxurious and nostalgic past. The menus offer a very interesting quality/price ratio.

For rail enthusiasts, Le Wagon Bleu restaurant in Paris (see *Secret bars and restaurants in Paris* in this series of guides) is also in an authentic Orient Express carriage.

## SIGHTS NEARBY

### LE MINIMUSÉE DES MINIATURES

**8**

7, rue de la République 06380 Sospel
- Tel: 04 93 04 16 53
- Open from Ascension (40 days after Easter) to end of September, 10.00–12.00 except Wednesday and Saturday
- Admission: €2, children and groups €1

This museum, a miniature annex of the restaurant carriage of the Orient Express, offers a network of electric trains on 220 m of rails.

### KNICKER BUTTONS IN CHURCH

**9**

Église Sancta-Maria-in-Albis
Place Brancion 06540 Breil-sur-Roya
- Open daily 10.00–12.00 and 14.30–18.00 (19.00 in summer)

Inside the parish church you need good eyesight to make out these little circles of mother-of-pearl decorating the marble balustrade where the worshippers kneel for communion. After a gang of church-robbers had passed that way, the people of Breil noticed that these precious ornaments had been stolen. They decided to fill the gaps with buttons, also made from mother-of-pearl, from the undergarments of a few pious parishioners prepared to make sacrifices for the integrity of their church.

# FORT SAINT-ROCH

RD2204, 06380 Sospel
- Tel. : 04 93 04 00 70
- Open 14.00–18.00 Saturday, Sunday and public holidays in April, May, June and October
- Daily except Monday from July to September
- Admission: €5

## The museum of the Maginot Line fortifications

Built in 1932, Saint-Roch fort was a veritable underground town that formed part of the famous Maginot Line. Today, visitors can appreciate exactly what it was intended for: to close off the Bévéra valley and stop armoured Italian trains from entering French territory.

Benefiting from the latest technological developments of the pre-war period, the fortified complex of Saint-Roch was armed with a 75 mm gun aimed at Sospel station, four blind mortars angled across the fort, rapid-fire machine guns and grenade launchers for use should the surroundings trenches be invaded by the enemy. 5,000 m³ of concrete and 385 tonnes of steel protected some 300 men who could be self-sufficient for three months. The tour, to a depth of 50 m, of the electricity generating, ventilation and air filtering rooms, the infirmary, kitchens, sleeping and sanitary quarters gives a better understanding of the difficult conditions the men lived under. At the end of a corridor that seems to stretch into infinity you go down a 45° slope to the ammunition dump, which leads up again to the gunners' room. Orders from the observation towers were transmitted by "parlophone", whose copper piping runs around the ceiling of the subterranean galleries.

## MAGINOT LINE

Constructed in the 1930s, the Maginot Line was a fortified defensive barrier covering a zone from the River Sarr (north-east France) to the Mediterranean. Only the Belgian and Swiss borders together with the gap at the Sarr were left unprotected, so that an invading German army would have to pass through one of these routes. The German army finally did invade via Belgium (which had opted for neutrality in 1936), where the defensive line stopped, thus outflanking the obstacle of the Maginot Line, as foreseen by the strategists, but with such speed and efficiency (blitzkrieg or lightning war), that all French defence plans were ruined. On the Italian front the defences showed their great strength, but the Franco-Italian armistice of June 1940 rapidly put an end to the fighting. The line was named after André Maginot, France's minister of War in 1929, the driving force behind its construction although that was principally carried out under Paul Painlevé.

# THE TOWER OF LUCÉRAM

⓫

Rue de la Tour
06440 Lucéram

*An
"open-throat"
tower*

Atypical rural village, clinging to the steep mountain slopes and bordered by the River Paillon, which flows into the sea at Nice, Lucéram was a long-time stage on the Salt Road (see page 222). The village has retained part of its ramparts and notably a strange tower, *ouverte à la gorge* (open-throat).

Although from beyond the ramparts there seems nothing odd about this tower, from the inside you can get a better look at the architectural defensive technique, which consisted in leaving a hollow space in the part of the tower overlooking the village under protection. This would stop would-be invaders from using the tower to attack the inner village while supplies of food or ammunition could still be delivered easily to the tower occupants. The tower is 15 m high and 4.10 m around the base.

### SIGHTS NEARBY

⓬

Lucéram church, dedicated to St Margaret, possesses some of the richest religious heritage of the region. The retable of St Anthony of Padua painted by Jean Canavesio is next to one of Louis Bréa's masterpieces, the retable of *St Margaret issant du dragon* [i.e. coming out of the dragon] in gold and silver. Among the curiosities, you can't fail to spot that the engraver of the door lintel between the building adjacent (now home to the Centre d'Interprétation du Patrimoine, concerned with village memories) and the church hadn't prepared his text, because twice he has had to finish his phrases on the line above.

# MUSÉE DES VIEUX OUTILS

**⑬**

Chapelle Saint-Jean, 06440 Lucéram
Details from tourist office
• Tel/Fax: 04 93 79 46 50
• E-mail: officedetourismedeluceram@wanadoo.fr
• Tél./fax : 04 93 79 46 50

*Wolves among the penitents*

The very beautiful village of Lucéram is pedestrian only, not because of any by-law but because of its *en crèche* arrangement, clinging to a rocky peak and accessible by a network of narrow alleys, steeply sloping, sometimes with steps and vaulted over.

In this way you reach St John's chapel, former meeting place of the Pénitents Blancs brotherhood (see page 89 for more on penitents). On the façade of the chapel you can see a faded fresco showing two penitents at the foot of a cross.

Inside the chapel, the Musée des Vieux Outils brings together several hundred implements used in the past for agricultural, artisanal or domestic work. There are tools for cropping vines and making wine, olive oil and lavender, for the distillery, from working the soil to the harvest. The most spectacular object is probably the [anti-]wolf collar, which was worn as a matter of course round the necks of sheep spending the nights outside at pasture. The wolf is a predator that takes its prey by the throat.

## SIGHTS NEARBY

### AN AXE SHARPENER

**⑭**

Rue Haute-de-la-Tour
06390 Berre-les-Alpes

The house of Richard Cairaschi at number 6 rue Haute-de-la-Tour bears an odd inscription calling the passer-by a *"coion"* (*couillon*, a wally, to put it politely). Almost opposite is the base of a chateau tower. Looking closer, you can see strange slits cut regularly in the stone, the function of which is not immediately obvious. In fact they are for sharpening the axes used since the 14th century by the villagers.

# MUSÉE DE LA VIGNE ET DU VIN

1, rue Scuderi, 06390 Contes
- Open second and fourth Sundays in the month, 10.30–12.30 and 14.00–17.00
- Annual closure November
- Admission: €1.50

*Wine cellar in a hidden grotto*

I n the depths of the wine cellar that the former notary of Contes, Maître Fossati, had built for himself, a concealed entrance gives access to an amazing grotto. The legal eagle, known as a lover of fine wines, had gathered in his cellar all the tools and implements needed for conditioning and conserving wine: barrels, casks, bottles, all arranged in a superb *vinothèque*. Right at the back of the cellar, a strange recess in the wall, which you'd hardly notice unless you were particularly looking for it, served as a discreet entrance to his tasting room. With a low ceiling and covered with wallpaper, giving an air both theatrical and artificial, the only furniture was a baroque table and two benches, all in pretty rock-work imitating plant formations. Hard to imagine at what times and with whom Maître Fossati shut himself up here. Perhaps his only companion was one of his precious bottles?

The Museum of Vine and Wine is now located in this series of caves. Rarely open, it displays the collection of specialized implements that the notary had collected.

## SIGHTS NEARBY

### CONTES MARTINET AND IRON MILL

Quartier La Laouza 06390 Contes
- Open every Saturday 9.30–12.30 and 14.00–17.00
- Annual closure November • Admission: €2

Unique in Alpes-Maritimes, Contes iron mill was built in the 16th century. Located near the river, it has been classified as a historic monument since 1979, one of the rare examples of such mills in the world still in working order. It was even in service until 1951. An iron mill is a forge that works by hydraulic energy. In the first place the water moves the bellows via a water jet pump. Put simply, the water rushes into a vertical column and air compressed by its weight is used to fan the flames. The key role is played by the *martinet* [blacksmith's hammer], the word used to describe the mills themselves. This *martinet*, ancestor of the power hammer, is in fact a huge iron weight of 45 kilos with a wooden handle lifted by the force of the water. Finally, the hydraulic energy turns a grindstone to sharpen tools. The Contes *martinet* produces mainly agricultural implements (axes, billhooks, scythes), the raw materials (iron and steel) being supplied from Nice.

# THE ENGRAVED STONE OF CASTEL

Mairie, 06390 Contes

**D**iscovered in 1972 in the walls of the former chateau, the Castel stone remains an enigma to scientists. Consisting of a block of very fine, flaky clay, it has a cross on one side (probably to consecrate it) and on the other a series of inscriptions comparable with those dating from the Bronze Age found in the

> *No light yet shed on the significance of inscriptions*

Vallée des Merveilles (site of rock engravings 80 km north of Nice).

In 1973, the Institut de Préhistoire et d'Archéologie des Alpes-Maritimes published a report* on the stone: 14 *cupules*** have never been deciphered, there being no proof that they are not natural formations. The most intriguing aspect of all this is a series of seven very distinctive characters that closely resemble the ancient scripts of the Mediterranean basin: proto-Sinaitic, Canaanian, Egyptian hieroglyphics, Phoenician, Greek and Etruscan have been recognized. Some characters also recall the runes found all over Europe between the 3rd and 19th centuries.

Even though it has not been possible to make coherent sense of the inscriptions to mean either plants, animals or people, experts think that this stone could have been engraved between the 4th and 17th centuries by a learned man who knew the ancient scripts.

You used to be able to study the stone (which was recycled in restoration work at the Castel (chateau) of Contes in the 17th century) in rue du Castel. Curiously, the owner sold it to the Musée des Merveilles at Tende. Although you can still see the original, the faithful reproduction on show at Contes town hall is very pleasing.

(*) Pierre Bodard and Jean-Marie Ricolfis, *Une pierre à gravures à Contes (Alpes-Maritimes)*, in *Mémoires*, Vol. XV, Institut de Préhistoire et d'Archéologie des Alpes-Maritimes, 1971–1972, pp. 39–43, two figures.

(**) *Cupule* : cup-shaped depression in stone, named after the scaly skin around certain seeds or nuts such as the chestnut.

## SIGHTS NEARBY

### THE CANDLE STONE

Rue du Fraou 06390 Contes

Discreetly indicated by a plaque fixed to the wall in rue du Fraou is a stone that was used to light the candles during auction sales. Used in the past for the attribution of olive oil mills, sales *à la bougie* (or *à la chandelle*) go back to the 15th century and still take place today. Candles with very short wicks are used which smoke when they burn down. After two candles are thus seen to have gone out, and nobody has bid during that time (15–30 seconds), the sale is closed. This system gives the last bidder the time to reflect before it's too late.

# PYRAMID OF THE RATAPIGNATA

Domaine de la Bastide, 06950 Falicon

**Access:** to reach the pyramid, leave your car at Aire-Saint-Michel. You can take either of two routes (on foot). **The first option** is the famous GR5 (Grande Randonnée or "Long Trek" 5), which starts right there at Aire-Saint-Michel and ends in the Netherlands. The path climbs upwards and under two high-voltage power lines after some 20 minutes' walk up the hill. Just before you go under the second power line, look to the right for a goat track, fairly faint, that goes straight up to the crest. The pyramid is just before the top.

**The alternative route** is to follow the D114 for 200 m and turn left towards the hamlet of Giaïnes. From there, take the road marked "Chemin des Ratapignata", a pretty and very steep track wrecked by mountain-bikers who have ripped out all the stone steps to ride down as they please. Because of this the ground is very slippery, consisting of small stones on which you could miss your footing, especially on the way down. In the same spirit, all the wooden signs put up by the local authorities have been sawn up for firewood ... After a good quarter of an hour's climb a ruin comes into view: take the path to the right marked out with round yellow bollards.

> *A mysterious pyramid*

Rather lost in the countryside, a mysterious pyramid, whose point has been partly worn away, opens onto a vertiginous chasm known as the "grotte du Mont-Chauve" or "grotte du Ratapignata" (*Nissart* for bat). Discovered in 1803 by Domenico Rossetti, an Italian lawyer, the cave takes its name from the birds who roost there.

The proximity of the chasm and the pyramid is certainly no coincidence. Although several hypotheses have been put forward, none has met with universal agreement. Was it to mark an underground temple dedicated to Mithra and built by the Roman soldiers garrisoned at Cimiez? A sign erected by the Templars to indicate the entrance to the cave, then sheltering a leper colony? A 19th-century aesthetic folly to keep alive the spirit of Egyptian expeditions?

The most recent and seemingly the most plausible hypothesis is simply that of a marker put up by the person who discovered the cave, Domenico Rossetti, so that he could spot the entrance from a distance and to consecrate the place. Note, by the way, that in the lawyer's detailed descriptions he never mentions a pyramid …

How far can you follow the subterranean galleries of the grotte des Ratapignata? Nobody knows because a dense underground water network hinders speleological explorations. It is known, on the other hand, that the hillside is riddled with subterranean passages, some of which emerge in the houses of Giaïnes.

## SIGHTS NEARBY

**THE PLASTIC CHAPEL WINDOWS** OF SAINT-MARTIN-DE-PEILLE ⑳
RD53 06440 Peille • Information on completion of work and future opening from Peille town hall • Tel: 04 93 91 71 71

Between La Turbie and Peille, the chapel of Saint-Martin-de-Peille, built by Guzzi in 1951, is worth a detour (even if when this guide is published the work is still ongoing and you can't get in). Its 1950s style and its canopy, a veritable concrete helmet as an extension of the roof, are surprising. Another original feature: the "stained-plastic" windows.

# SANCTUARY OF NOTRE-DAME-DE-LAGHET

Sanctuaire Notre-Dame-de-Laghet 06340 La Trinité
- Open all year 7.00–21.00
- Museum 15.30–17.00 (except Tuesday)
- Tel: 04 92 41 50 50 • Fax: 04 92 41 50 59
- http://nice.cef.fr/laghet • E-mail: sanctuairelaghet@free.fr

*Exceptional ex-votos*

Inaugurated in the 17th century, the sanctuary of Notre-Dame-de-Laghet has an exceptional collection of over 4,000 ex-votos distributed between the cloister, the church and, for the most precious among them, the museum. Unfortunately, the sanctuary was pillaged during the Revolution and since then the oldest ex-votos are late 18th-century.

Among the most interesting pieces of the museum is the ex-voto relating Constantin Spinelli's accident. When he was in a coma after falling from a train, the Virgin appeared to him and said: "The hour has not yet come for you to die, Spinelli, convert!" A militant communist, he and his entire family converted to Christianity but he didn't reveal his vision of Mary until he was on his deathbed.

The story of the sanctuary of Notre-Dame-de-Laghet goes back to the 17th century when Don Jacques Fighiera, a priest from the nearby village of Èze, paid for the restoration of the dilapidated chapel of the hamlet of Laghet. In 1652, three miracles brought fame to the modest place of worship: Hyacinte Casanova, a leprosy sufferer who doctors had given up as lost, was suddenly cured after coming to Laghet; the son of Anne Giongona, captured by barbarian pirates, was freed at the very moment when his mother, in novena* at the chapel, thought she saw him; finally, Marie Aicard, an epileptic possessed by a demon, found peace and serenity after an exorcism carried out by Don Fighiera.

The priest therefore placed in the Laghet chapel a statue of the Virgin Mary that he had had carved from a tree on his land, which became the object of pilgrim worship. Over time, the reputation of Laghet attracted more and more supplicants hoping for miracles, which increased in their turn, until the Bishop of Nice decided to build a sanctuary to welcome the faithful. It was consecrated on 21 November 1656.

(*)A form of worship in the Roman Catholic Church with special prayers on nine successive days.

## WHAT IS AN EX-VOTO?

The ex-voto is a mark of gratitude addressed to a saint (often to the Holy Virgin) after a "miracle" has been performed. These may involve shipwrecks, domestic accidents or illnesses, where a request for intercession by a saint has led to a positive outcome. The term "ex-voto" is an abbreviation of the Latin phrase *ex voto suscepto* [from the vow made].

# LE CHATEAU DE L'AIGUETTA

Quartier de l'Aiguetta 06360 Eze-Village • Access: from the village car park, take the road opposite which leads to La Turbie via the Grande Corniche (highest of the three tiers of roads between Nice and Menton). The best view of the chateau, although behind some trees, is from the fire station.

I f you happen to visit Èze on a day when storms are threatening, the sight of the Aiguetta chateau will convince you that you've left the Côte d'Azur for an impromptu stay in Scotland. The building with its towers, crenellations and imitation stonework, is really impressive and totally unexpected in this location.

*A Scottish manor on the Riviera*

Begun in 1899, built higher in 1901 and enlarged in the first quarter of the 20th century, the chateau is now left to ruin. It was built by the nephew of Alfred, Lord Tennyson, renowned English poet (1809–1892) in a style worthy of Disneyland. Walt Disney himself has stayed in the village of Èze. Maybe that's where he found his inspiration for the castle in *Sleeping Beauty*?

## SIGHTS NEARBY

### SOUVENIRS OF THE NAVY
Quai Courbet 06230 Villefranche-sur-Mer

On quai Courbet, which runs alongside the streets and alleys of the old town of Villefranche-sur-Mer, wall-plaques recall the strategic role of this port during the Cold War. Villefranche was in fact the home port of certain ships of the US Navy's 6th Fleet in the Mediterranean. Relations between the military and the local residents were obviously cordial and the plaque offered by the destroyer *USS Springfield* is particularly appealing: "In recognition of the warm hospitality offered by the people of Villefranche during the six years we were anchored here."

### THE PRAYER OF THE TURKISH PRISONERS:
### AN ENGRAVED STONE LOST AND FOUND BY CHANCE
Mairie. Citadelle. 06230 Villefranche-sur-Mer

In the ruins of the lazaretto (isolation hospital), when mechanical diggers left in 1960, a chance find was made of a stone with an Arabic prayer inscribed on it. Classified as a historic artefact in 1911, it had gone missing …
Originally the stone probably came from the prayer room of the jailhouse reserved for Muslim prisoners. The Turks captured at sea or on the North African coasts were imprisoned or, when the need arose, served as galley slaves. Note that until recently the word "Turk" was used to describe the inhabitants of Palestine or the Maghreb as well as those of the Ottoman Empire. The text would probably have been engraved on the stone in the 18th century by a group of prisoners who prayed to God to deliver them from Hell. A translation was provided by Marie-Madeleine Viré in the Arab studies journal *Arabica*. After giving thanks to God, the text specifically asks Him to free them "from the hands of their wicked enemies". The stone is now in the entrance hall of Villefranche town hall, in the citadel.

## ANGELS OF THE SEA AT THE MUSÉE OCÉANOGRAPHIQUE ㉕

Avenue Saint-Martin MC 98000 Monaco
• Tel: + 377 93 15 36 00
• www.oceano.mc • E-mail: resa@oceano.mc
• Open from January to March 10.00–18.00, April to June 9.30–19.00, July and August 9.30–19.30, September 9.30–19.00 and October to December 10.00–18.00. • Admission: adults € 11, children (6 to 18 years), students, disabled people € 6. Children under 6 free.

*The origin of Nice's "Baie des Anges" is in Monaco*

**K**nown throughout the world, Baie des Anges bathes the city of Nice and extends from Cap d'Antibes (or some say from the mouth of the Var) to Cap de Nice. A legend explains the name of the bay thus: the body of St Réparate, beheaded by the Romans in Palestine in 250, had been set adrift in a boat and brought by the angels to the shores of the bay in question. Her relics are now in Nice's Sainte-Réparate cathedral.

Alexis de Jussieu in his poem *Adam et Ève*, published in 1856, tells when the two human beings were banished from the Garden of Eden, they were carried by angels to the surroundingss of what is now Nice. Implicit in this is the understanding that the place was just as beautiful as their lost paradise ... In fact, the bay was named by fishermen who brought up in their nets a vast number of angelfish or angel sharks, of the species *squatina angelus* or *squatina squatina*. This type of monkfish, which has now abandoned the shores that bear its name, is harmless and can be recognized by its wing-like pectoral and pelvic fins.

Although the Musée d'Histoire Naturelle de Nice has a fine stuffed example of the angel shark, over a metre long, it is for the time being in the reserve and not on show.

To see a (stuffed) angelfish today, you'll need to go to the Musée Océanographique de Monaco, to the applied oceanography room, known as *salle de la baleine*, where the common angelfish *squatina squatina* is exhibited, caught in the Gulf of Porto on 4 October 1950 by HRH Prince Rainier III himself. It only survived six days in the aquarium after its capture.

# BOUNDARY STONES

**(26)**

## BETWEEN THE PRINCIPALITY OF MONACO AND THE HOUSE OF SAVOY

- Borne de la Mairie (**left-hand photo**)
Mairie de Monaco Place de la Mairie 98000 Monaco
- Borne de l'escalier Sainte-Cécile (**centre photo**)
Place du Crédit-Lyonnais 98000 Monaco
- Borne de Moneghetti (**right-hand photo**)
Chemin de La Turbie 98000 Monaco

> *Up to the stones, it's Monaco ...*

Monaco still harbours on its territory three boundary stones, discreet but visible, each bearing the cross of Savoy. In 1828 they indicated the limit of the principality's lands (protectorate of the Kingdom of Sardinia) and those of the House of Savoy.

The first stone is the only one to have been moved. It was originally at Roquebrune-Cap-Martin. Roquebrune and Menton formed part of the principality at the time and allied themselves with France in 1848. The stone is now in the courtyard of Monaco's town hall. To see it you have to ask permission from the doorman to go inside. As the building is right in the centre of the old town of Monaco (The Rock), this is an opportunity to stroll the narrow streets and browse the many shops, visit the cathedral (with the tomb of Princess Grace), admire the princely palace or watch the inevitable changing of the guard (at 11.55 precisely).

The second stone is at the present boundary between Monaco and the French commune of Beausoleil, at the foot of the Sainte-Cécile stairway. You are then in Monte-Carlo, in sight of the casino and the Hôtel de Paris where the staff waits for the Rolls.

The third and last stone lets you escape from the usual Monaco tours because it stands opposite Moneghetti church. Near the Jardin-Exotique, Moneghetti is a magnificent district offering an unbeatable view of the bay. The Free Commune of Moneghetti organizes regular events that enliven this rarely visited part of Monaco.

# HOW TO CROSS THE PRINCIPALITY IN 17 MINUTES ON FOOT

It's a mystery to nobody that the main problem with the principality for walkers is its steep slopes that transform any walk, lengthwise, into a sometimes painful trial. Moreover the traffic is often dense, as it is elsewhere on the Côte d'Azur, and in the high season completely saturated. Here therefore is a route that will let you, in record time and with moderate physical effort, go for a drink in the port or watch the changing of the guard. All this and an idea for free parking thrown in …

*Underground Monaco*

First take the middle road of the three corniches. Remember that three roads, apart from the motorway, link Nice with Monaco, the *corniche inférieure*, the *moyenne corniche* and the Grande Corniche or *corniche supérieure*. Park near the sign marking the exit from the commune of La Turbie, followed by a sign for Beausoleil (n°1). The first public lift on your journey is to the left (facing Italy), in the Patio Palace building (n°2). Inside, change to the "*panoramique*" lift, which will take you to the exit of the building on avenue Hector-Otto (n°3).

Go left on leaving the building as far as the hairpin bend (n°4), where you'll find the third lift on your tour, still in avenue Hector-Otto, in the Magnolias building (n°5). This lift takes you to the boulevard du Jardin-Exotique (n°6) where you head right for the next lift. Be careful not to fall into the trap of entering the lift in a little tower (n°7) on the beach side of the boulevard, but rather take the one inside the building opposite (n°8). You'll emerge in the car park of the Jardin-Exotique on boulevard de Belgique (n°9). Go left. There the longest part of the walk awaits you but it's all on the level (n°10). Allow a good five minutes to come back to the last public lift of the trip, the one that takes you to place Sainte-Dévote, at sea level, in the port of Monaco (n°12). In the underground passage (n°11), avoid a further diversion by ignoring the signs for Gare de Monaco.

* The numbers indicated in the text correspond with those on the photos in the mosaic..

### DEUX PAYS POUR UN MÊME BOULEVARD

• Boulevard du Général-Leclerc
06240 Beausoleil
• Boulevard de France
98000 Monaco

The French commune of Beausoleil is so closely adjacent to Monaco that sometimes you change country without noticing. The most striking example is the "boulevard de France" on the Monaco side, with even numbers (on the right going up the road), and "boulevard du Général-Leclerc" on the French side, with odd numbers (on the left going up). Although along the boulevard, the buildings and offices on opposite sides are similar, they have drastically different tax regimes ...

### PRINCIPALITY OF MONACO

The Principality of Monaco (1.95 km$^2$) is the second smallest state in the world, after the Vatican (0.44 km$^2$). It holds the world record for population density with 16,000 residents per km$^2$. Of the 31,000 residents counted in 2006, only 3,000 are Monegasque. 125 different nationalities rub shoulders in the tiny territory and, among the many foreigners, most are French, who make up 47% of the population. To take advantage of the coveted Monegasque nationality, you have to have lived in the principality for over 10 years since the age of 18, not be a civil servant or have military obligations in another country, and renounce your former nationality. These criteria for admission are essential but not sufficient, as the final decision lies with the prince alone. Official languages are French and Monegasque (or Ligurian Monegasque as it's similar to the dialect of the Ligurian coast of northwest Italy). Monaco is a constitutional monarchy with a prince as head of state and a minister of state nominated by the prince with the accord of France.

The Grimaldi family's authority over Monaco was recognized in 1314. It has continued to the present day, with the exception of a brief interlude between 1793 and 1814 during which Monaco was annexed to France, under the name of Fort Hercule. At the Congress of Vienna in 1815, the town was placed under the protection of the Kingdom of Sardinia until 1860, and it regained its sovereignty in 1861. The French communes of Menton and Roquebrune (now Roquebrune-Cap-Martin) used to form part of the principality. In 1848, they rose up and proclaimed themselves free towns. They were reattached to France by the treaty of 1861.

# WALK ALONG
## THE FORMER TRAMWAY LINKING LA TURBIE TO MONACO

**28**

- Place de la Crémaillère 98000 Monaco
- Rue de la Crémaillère 06240 Beausoleil
- Ancienne voie de la Crémaillère 06240 Beausoleil
- Chemin de la Crémaillère 06320 La Turbie

*A
nostalgic but
invigorating walk*

Here's a nostalgic and healthy way of discovering the surroundingss of Monaco: a walk along the former tramway that used to link Monaco with La Turbie.

Before the communes of Cap-d'Ail and Beausoleil came into being, the La Turbie authorities had the idea of opening up the highest part of the village for tourism. The commune did after all have on its patch the remarkable Roman site of Trophée des Alpes. For this reason, 2.6 km of track was laid on which the first rack-and-pinion tram, pulled by a steam locomotive, was inaugurated on 10 February 1894. On 8 March 1932, the train heading upwards suddenly ran backwards at an ever-increasing speed that nothing could halt. The drama caused several deaths and put a definitive end to the tramway business. Even though there is now talk of a possible reopening of this means of transport, highly developed in Europe, pressure from real estate interests seems to be too powerful to let the project go ahead.

To go on foot from Monaco to La Turbie while taking in the remaining traces of the tramway, set off from place de la Crémaillère in Monaco. Just above the square, a nameless road belonging to the commune of Beausoleil is dominated by two enormous pillars, no less than the foundations of the former terminus. Take the Riviera steps, which link Monaco directly with the Riviera Palace. From this prestigious hotel (now under co-ownership so that you can visit some sections through Beausoleil tourist office), rue de la Crémaillère to the left will take you as far as the EDF power plant. You can clearly see the green cutting that the tram followed but not the inscription on the former station, "Monte-Carlo supérieur". Once on the middle cornice, take the old paved road of la Crémaillère until it turns into a dirt track. You reach the village of La Turbie by following the chemin de la Crémaillère where, here and there, a few iron rails from the old line emerge from the ground.

## MONTE-CARLO OR MONACO?

If there is any confusion between the two places in the minds of those that don't live in the area, this will clear it up: Monte-Carlo is just one of the six districts that make up the Principality of Monaco. It was named "Mount Charles" in honour of Prince Charles III of Monaco.

# CABIN OF LE CORBUSIER

Promenade Le Corbusier 06190 Roquebrune-Cap-Martin
• Visits arranged by Roquebrune-Cap-Martin tourist office, Tuesday and Fridays
at 10.00 • Admission: €8 adults, €5 students, children under 12 free
• Office de tourisme de Roquebrune-Cap-Martin
218, avenue Aristide-Briand 06190 Roquebrune-Cap-Martin
• Tel: 04 93 35 62 87 • E-mail: otroquebrunecm@ifrance.com

T he tour of the *château* (as he liked to call it) of the celebrated architect Le Corbusier is an extremely pleasurable occasion, not only because of the beauty of the site, but especially for the architectural technique employed here without restrictions.

*The smallest dwelling classed as a historic monument in France*

In the 1930s, Le Corbusier began to spend time in the Roquebrune region, more accurately in villa E-1027 belonging to the decorator and architect Eileen Gray (the villa is currently being restored and you can't visit it). The idea came to him to build a "summer cabin". He designed it in three-quarters of an hour.

The result, constructed in Corsican pine, was a cabin of modest dimensions (366 cm by 366 cm, 226 cm high), the proportions worked out according to Le Corbusier's "Modulor" norms (proportions based on the human body), where in particular he had to be able to touch the ceiling by raising his arms above his head. He often went there in summer from 1952 onwards.

In such a confined space, everything was of course thought out for maximum practicality. Le Corbusier designed (and sometimes executed) all the details of the interior fittings: a bed, a washroom and carefully designed mirrored sections on the inside of the shutters. The walls served as table or chest of drawers and the ceiling as storage space.

A visit to the cabin includes the five camping units, installed nearby, which were also conceived and funded by Le Corbusier.

## SIGHTS NEARBY

### ROQUEBRUNE'S FALSE TRIUMPHAL ARCH
Avenue Churchill

Whatever it may look like, the entrance to the former property of Clos du Cap-Martin is not a Roman triumphal arch. Blending in perfectly with the mausoleum built 2,000 years earlier, it was added in 1882 in the antique style.

### LUMONE'S MAUSOLEUM: A ROMAN TOMB IN THE TOWN CENTRE
Corner of avenue Paul-Doumer and avenue Bedoux

Difficult to find even when you're looking out for it, the tomb of Lumone (a Roman nobleman) was made accessible to the public in 1950. In a square where it passes unnoticed, the monument is worth a look: it consists of a Roman funerary enclosure dating from between 100 BC and 40 BC. Richly decorated with black and white stones together with red bricks, all in diamond or chequerboard shapes, it contains hidden niches where traces of frescoes can be seen. Originally, the tomb was by the side of the Via Aurelia, the route that in antiquity linked Rome to Gaul.

# VILLA FONTANA ROSA

3, avenue Blasco-Ibañez
06500 Menton
• Open only for guided tours run by the Heritage service on Fridays (except public holidays) at 10.00 (see page 49) • Booking on site.

*A villa full of novelists*

Even though the building is still being restored and can only be seen as part of a guided tour, villa Fontana Rosa won't disappoint lovers of the unusual. Constructed from 1922 until his death in 1928 by Vicente Blasco Ibañez, a Spanish novelist originally from Valencia where he was the subject of extraordinary devotion, the house was intended to be a writer's haven.

Over a period of seven years, Ibañez commissioned bronze statues of his favourite writers from the Russian sculptor Léopold Bernstamm. Balzac, Dickens, Zola, Hugo, Dostoyevsky, Flaubert, Boccaccio, Tolstoy, Goethe, Poe, Stendhal as well as Beethoven, his preferred musician, thus took their places in the park. His compatriot Cervantes merited special treatment: the rotunda dedicated to him is entered by a monumental stairway and, below the arched colonnade, are 100 ceramic tiles made at Manises, near Valence, telling the Don Quixote story in a splendidly original fashion

The library from which part of the 500,000 books have been saved is also in a very dilapidated state but in the long term should be the heart of the future activities planned for the villa. It will indeed be a literary villa where the public can come and borrow books to read in the garden.

## SIGHTS NEARBY

### HOMAGE TO TWO STALLHOLDERS: PLAQUES TO LA TATOUNE AND LA TAVINA

Halle municipale
Rue des Marins 06500 Menton

A unique and highly congenial initiative to pay homage to two market sellers of vegetables and of *socca** and *pichade***! This is how two plaques fixed to the wall of Menton's covered market honour the memory of Madame Octavie Orengo, known as la Tavina, and of Madame Joséphine Viegl, known as la Tatoune.

\* *Socca* is a large thin pancake, made from chick-pea flour with the addition of a little olive oil, water and salt. It is cooked on copper plates in the oven (and according to a disappearing tradition, over a wood fire). The sellers cut it up with a spatula and add a little pepper on request. A speciality of Nice and Menton, it is eaten as an aperitif with a glass of wine or while strolling through the streets of Menton or the old town of Nice. *Socca* shouldn't be reheated but eaten fresh from the oven.

\*\* *Pichade*, a speciality of the Menton region, is a dough base to which is added tomatoes, onions, garlic and small black olives.

# THE INSCRIBED STONE OF RUE PIETRA-SCRITTA   ③④

Rue Pietra-Scritta, beside number 38
06500 Menton

*A street whose name suits it well*

Fixed to the rocks in the centre of the roadway (the street name, *pietra scritta* in the Menton dialect, means "inscribed stone"), a marble plaque bears a Latin inscription that may be translated thus: "Antoine I ordered the widening of this roadway through the rocks to facilitate his travels and for the benefit of his people. Year 1717." Prince of Monaco, Duke of Valentinois, Marquis of Les Baux, Count of Carladès and Lord of Menton, Antoine I was also Lord of Roquebrune from 1701 to 1731.

It was in 1346 that the Grimaldi family acquired the seigneury of Menton (followed by that of Roquebrune). These lords' domains, together with that of Monaco, constituted the territory of the principality from 1633 to 1861. There was however a break in this arrangement as Menton was annexed to the first *département* of Alpes-Maritimes set up between 1793 and 1814. In 1860, the population of Menton (as well as Roquebrune and Nice), voted by a crushing majority to link their destiny with that of France. A last Italian phase took place during the Second World War, when Mussolini's troops invaded the town.

## LA SALLE DES MARIAGES OF THE MAIRIE DE MENTON ③⑤

Hôtel de Ville 17, rue de la République 06500 Menton
• Tel: 04 92 10 50 29
• Open daily except Saturday, Sunday and public holidays, 8.30–12.30 and 14.00–17.00.
• Admission: adults €1.50. Groups and students (under 25): €1.15. Free for under 18s.

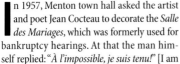

> *Marry amidst Cocteau's decorations*

In 1957, Menton town hall asked the artist and poet Jean Cocteau to decorate the *Salle des Mariages*, which was formerly used for bankruptcy hearings. At that the man himself replied: "*À l'impossible, je suis tenu!*" [I am obliged to do the impossible!]. Opened on 25 March 1958, the room has become a symbol and encourages some people to get married again and again … And therein lies the problem, as requests for marriages ceremonies there now flood in from all around the world.

Entering the room is a magical experience because, other than being original, the artist made no attempt to desanctify the marital vows. On the contrary he has gone a long way towards emphasize the sumptuous traditional aspects of the ceremony without forgetting a touch of fantasy: the seats with their velvet upholstery are wedded with a leopard-skin carpet. Cocteau also asked that Mendelssohn's "Wedding March" should be played at the end of each ceremony.

The fresco on the main wall shows the spouses: the bride, with her Mentonaise headdress; the groom, with his fisherman's cap, eye in the shape of a fish. On the right-hand wall, they are leaving for the honeymoon, but seem to be nervous! And on the left wall is one of the artist's recurring themes, the death of Eurydice.

Even the ceiling was decorated by Cocteau who took the opportunity for a "alpine cure on the scaffolding".

He eventually summed up his artistic efforts at Menton town hall in the following phrase: "*Voilà l'ensemble qui m'aide à rendre moins sévère la rigueur du code Napoléon*" [Here is the setting that helps me lessen the severity of the Napoleonic Code].

### SIGHTS NEARBY

### LE MUSÉE JEAN COCTEAU ③⑥
Bastion du Vieux-Port 06500 Menton
• Tel: 04 93 57 72 30
• Admission: €3. Groups: €2.25

Jean Cocteau always held a special relationship with Menton. The town bastion, the port's defensive fortifications dating from the 17th century, would become his memorial, and it was also his last work. He conceived the interior restoration himself, designing floor mosaics and wrought-iron windows. The museum is entirely the work of the poet and a testament to his artistic achievement.

## CITRUS TREES OF THE JARDIN DU PALAIS CARNOLÈS

3, avenue de la Madone 06500 Menton
• Open all year except Tuesdays and public holidays, 10.00–12.00 and 14.00–18.00
• Admission free
• Guided tour run by the Heritage service as part of events programme (€5)
• To buy kumquats: central market in Halle Municipale, Rue des Marins 06500 Menton

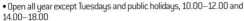

**Taste the smallest citrus fruit in the world at Menton**

Little known in France but grown at Menton, the kumquat is the smallest citrus fruit in the world: no more than 5 cm in diameter. Its skin, which looks rather like orange peel, is edible and it tastes mildly acid and bitter, which lends it great originality. The name of the tree, also kumquat (*Fortunella japonica*), is from the Cantonese for "golden orange" or "little golden citrus". In France, the fruit is grown in Corsica as well as around Menton.

Other than the kumquats, the garden of Palais Carnolès possesses the largest collection of citrus trees in Europe: 137 varieties (lemon, orange, mandarin, clementine, citron, bermagot orange).

A word to foodies: at Menton and on the Italian Riviera, an amazing spiny artichoke is cultivated that has to be cleaned and consumed with care, since the spines are so formidably sharp. It is eaten raw, seasoned with a trickle of the unbeatable local olive oil.

MAISON DU PATRIMOINE
5, rue Ciapetta , 06500 Menton
• Tel. : 04 92 10 33 66 • E-mail : josiane.tricotti@ville-menton.fr
• Open Monday to Friday 8.00–12.00 and 14.00–17.00

### SIGHTS NEARBY

### WALLED GARDEN OF PEYRONNET

Private garden: visits by appointment only
Avenue Aristide-Briand 06500 Menton
• Further details: service du Patrimoine, Palais d'Adhémar de Lantagnac
• 24, rue Saint-Michel
• Tel: 04 92 10 97 10

Since 1915 the Waterfield family has maintained and developed a very original garden whose pride and joy is a "water stairway", a succession of square basins the last of which is no less than the Mediterranean. Also ask to see the suggestive fresco in which the head of the household appears twice …

# NICE

BOULET
TIRAT PER LA FLOTA TU[...]
EN 1543
A L'ASSEDI DE N[...]
DOUN SI DESTING[...]
CATARINA SÉGUR[...]
L'EROUINA NISSA[...]

# THE CANNONBALL OF THE OLD TOWN

At the corner of rue Droite and rue de la Loge
Vieux-Nice

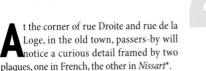

*Turkey sizzlers*

At the corner of rue Droite and rue de la Loge, in the old town, passers-by will notice a curious detail framed by two plaques, one in French, the other in *Nissart\**.

This authentic cannonball, embedded in the wall, was fired in the 16th century from one of the ships of the Ottoman fleet commanded by the famous Barbarossa (Redbeard), which laid siege to the town in 1543. As the explanatory text makes clear, this siege gave one citizen, Catherine Ségurane, the chance to distinguish herself. When the invaders attacked the town on 15 August, the heroic Niçoise destroyed the Turkish flag with her *battoir* [piece of wood on a handle, for beating linen clean]. It is said that on lifting her skirts and revealing herself to the enemy, she provoked their hasty retreat. Since then, each year around 8 September (the feast of Catarina Segurana) and on 25 December, Nice pays tribute to its heroine.

At the time, Nice and Savoy formed part of the vast Holy Roman Empire of Charles V. After the emperor's armies had taken Milan, the French king Francis I responded by attacking Savoy, whose duke Charles III left Turin and took refuge in Nice with his wife, son and the Holy Shroud. The French having sided with the Turks, it was only natural that Barbarossa would find himself laying siege to Nice …

The resistance of the population, of which Catherine Ségurane became the symbol, as well as the solidity of the castle ramparts, saved the town. On 8 September, the arrival of the army raised by Charles III forced the retreat of the Ottoman fleet, which passed the winter at Toulon. The thwarted attack of 15 August and the liberation of 8 September took on a miraculous aspect, all the more so as these dates correspond with two feast days of the Holy Virgin. Is it not said, moreover, that she appeared in the sky above the town and enveloped it in her cloak to protect it from the Turkish cannonballs … ?

(\*) Nissart (Niçard, local name) or Niçois (French name) is not a dialect but a language descended from the original Occitan (*langue d'oc*) of the Middle Ages, which referred to the use of *oc* for "yes" (from Latin *hoc*), in contrast to the French language (*langue d'oïl*), which used *oïl* (modern *oui*) for "yes" (from Latin *hoc ille*). Like Provençal, *Nissart* has a grammar, a dictionary and is taught at school to *baccalauréat* level and at university.

> Other cannonballs can be found in Nice. Three are very easy to spot, in place Garibaldi, on the façade of the chapel of Très-Saint-Sépulcre-des-Pénitents-Bleus.

### SIGHTS NEARBY

The church of Saint-Martin-Saint-Augustin retains, left of the choir, a curious medieval marble plaque (1444), which came from the former church. It was found in the stonecutters' chapel and represents a Virgin with Child surrounded by a dedication in Gothic lettering. Most surprising, however, is one of the earliest known and dated depictions of modern chisels, below on the left.

# THE NEIGHBOURHOODS OF THE OLD TOWN ❸

Le Vieux-Nice

I n the former "postal" system of the old town of Nice, the streets were nameless. The blocks of houses (*îlots*), were dedicated to a saint. So people lived in îlot Saint-Pierre or îlot Sainte-Anne. There still remain a few rare reminders of this time. At the corner

*When letters were addressed to blocks*

of rues Alexandre-Mari and Raoul-Bosio, for example, a medallion representing St François de Paule armed with his stick announces the *îlot* that used to be dedicated to him. Born in the village of Paule in Calabria (Italy) in 1416, he founded the Minimes order.

At the corner of rues de la Poissonnerie and Barilleri, you can also see the inscription "S Maria Madalena" carved in the stone, which clearly indicates the former *îlot* dedicated to St Mary Magdalene.

## SIGHTS NEARBY ❹

Inside the galleries of Les Ponchettes and La Marine, the town's exhibition spaces, the stone columns are numbered in a curious way. They mark the stalls of the former fish market that used to be held there.

Alongside the quai des Etats-Unis, a hoist lies on the beach, left there by some miracle as a reminder that fishermen dragged their boats up onto the shore using such implements.

### THE HANGING GATE ❺
Cours Saleya

On the gatepost of one of the gates linking cours Saleya to rue des Ponchettes, a Latin inscription has given this passage the erroneous nickname "La Porte des Pendus" [The Hanging Gate]. It reads: *Opt. Regi Carolo felici adventanti Nicaeenses portam et corda pandunt.* Although the last two words of the text evoke the hangman's rope, in fact it concerns a message of welcome translated thus: "In homage to the passage of the good king Charles-Félix, the people of Nice open their heart and their gate." This text recalls the visit of the King of Sardinia, Nice having been under Sardinian sovereignty from 1814 to 1860. But if the gate is ominously associated today with hanging, this is not without reason in the Niçois collective memory. From 1792 to 1814, after the invasion of the County of Nice by the French army, rebels known as Barbets took up arms against the occupying forces and stood up to the French. The reprisals were pitiless and many of the rebels were hung or shot without trial. Le Saut des Français [Frenchmen's Leap], a site near Duranus, is so-called in memory of this troubled time of summary executions.

(\*) "Barbets" was an insulting name given in the 16th and 17th centuries to the Vaudois of Dauphiné province, because of their long beards.

# CONCEALED AIR CONDITIONING OF THE OLD TOWN ⑥

> *Metal grilles, stairways, courtyards, shutters, are not only decorative*

**D**espite what you might think, gates, stairways, little courtyards and shutters are not only decorative: they are fabulous elements of the "passive" air conditioning of the neighbourhood. In summer, walking among these old buildings, you are indeed surprised at the protection they provide from the heatwave overpowering the rest of the town.

This can be explained partly because the area had been constructed taking account of the nearby sources of cool air: the River Paillon (now covered), the sea and the hill of the Château. The streets had thus been oriented towards them, creating a refreshing breeze that circulated through the alleyways, blew through the houses (see below for how this is done) and filtered out through the roofs.

Then, the openings decorated with wrought-iron grilles, found above most doors and fitted with security bars, are in fact air inlets. Moreover, the corridors often have a vaulted ceiling that directs cooler air towards the staircase. This air is also captured by the precisely calculated angle of the slats of the very typical Niçois shutters: they can be adapted to the strength and direction of the breeze. The trapped current of air will then find its way through the communicating rooms of the house and leave by the small interior courtyards that serve as air vents. A final detail: the communicating doors between rooms have non-symmetrical hinges, which means they can be left open without slamming in the breeze. You can see a fine example on the second floor of the Lascaris Palace, built by the Lascaris-Vintimille family. A listed historic monument, it is now a museum run by the City of Nice.

## THE TRUE STORY OF THE FALSE DOOR
Passage between rue de la Boucherie and boulevard Jean-Jaurès

Just like the citizens of Lyons with their *traboules* (private passageways or corridors in buildings), serving as shortcuts between two streets, those of Nice are in the habit of using the door of a building that on one side gives onto the banks of the Paillon (the covered river) and on the other onto rue de la Boucherie in the heart of the old town. After the war, the local authority regularized things by transforming this door into a proper passageway, high and wide. Its name, unusual and secretive at the time, is now engraved for everybody to see on one of the pillars: "false door"…

## CULT OF ST RITA ❼

L'église de l'Annonciation
1, rue de la Poissonnerie
• Open 7.00–12.00 and 14.30–18.30

### *The saint of lost causes*

In a parish dedicated to Saint-Jacques-le-Majeur (San-Giaume to the Niçois) since the Middle Ages, the Church of the Annunciation has been rebuilt twice: in the 17th century, on the site of the religious building that it replaced, then after the fire of 1834. Despite the church's official name, the local people know it mainly as the church of St Rita, whose cult is observed in the first chapel to the left and, especially, in the sacristy.

The patron of lost causes, St Rita is shown with a nail in her forehead, beaded with blood. Even if you are prepared for it, the incessant stream of women who come here, often in pairs, is astonishing. Remember to leaf through the visitors' book, which contains requests that are surreal, highly unlikely and often moving.

---

**ST RITA**

A contemporary of Joan of Arc, Margarita Mancini (Rita is of course short for Margarita) was born in 1381 at Roccaporena in Umbria (Italy). She was noted from childhood following an incident that was taken as a miracle: a swarm of bees flew into her open mouth without doing her any harm.

Married to please her parents, she lost her husband and two sons who died a violent death. She then devoted herself to what had always been her vocation: the love of Christ. Despite her widow's status preventing her from entering a convent, she was called by the Augustine sisterhood. Anything that was asked of her came to pass, her reputation steadily grew and she quickly became the advocate of lost causes and healer of smallpox. As she was praying in the church, a thorn from Christ's crown fell down and pierced her forehead. A pestilential smell later came from the infected wound and she was isolated in a cell, where she died with her face restored to a supernatural beauty, while the perfume of roses spread around the convent. Her embalmed body remains perfectly preserved at Cascia, near her home village.

In Paris, two churches bear her name, the most notable in the 15th *arrondissement* where twice a year remarkable masses are held to bless animals (see the *Secret Paris* guidebook in this series).

## THE TOMB OF EMIL JELLINEK: A MARQUED SPOT

Cimetière du Château
Allée François-Aragon

Those who are brave enough to climb the steps leading to the chateau and main cemetery of Nice are in for a surprise. An extraordinary panorama opens out towards the Alps, the Baie des Anges and the Promenade des Anglais. The cemetery receives a huge number of visitors every day from the Italian side of the mountain, who meet up

> **What Mercedes owes to a child of 11 ...**

at the tomb of Garibaldi, even though he has not occupied it for some time. The epitaph is unbeatable: *À la mémoire impérissable du plus illustre Niçois* [To the imperishable memory of the most illustrious Niçois]. The tombs of Léon Gambetta and of Gaston Leroux,* creator of Rouletabille, can also be seen there.

The most unusual mausoleum is nevertheless that of Emil Jellinek (on the highest level of the cemetery). A plaque in front of it explains: "He brilliantly contributed to the development of this new method of transport. His family is intimately linked with the name Daimler-Benz AG. In 1901, he gave the name of his daughter Mercedes to the products of Daimler Motoren Gessellschaft".

Jellinek, consul of the Austro-Hungarian Empire and a wealthy businessman based in Nice, was a faithful client of Daimler and their early motor-cars. A keen driver, he organized several races around Nice in which he took part. Witness to a tragic accident during the Nice-La Turbie rally (see page 66), he asked Gottlieb Daimler to use specifications that he had drawn up himself, based on improving security and lowering the centre of gravity of the car. He agreed to help fund the development of this vehicle on condition that it bore the name of his 11-year-old daughter: Mercedes.

On 21 March 1899, at the Nice-Magagnosc-Nice rally, Jellinek put money on his Daimler which for the first time started the race under the name Mercedes. Two years later, the whole Daimler fleet adopted the name. By borrowing his daughter's name, he unknowingly gave birth to an automobile marque of international renown.

The tomb had been neglected for many years and it is said that the company of the three-pointed star had been called on recently to refurbish the memory of the man to whom it owes so much.

*French novelist best known for *Phantom of the Opera*, who also wrote a series featuring amateur detective Joseph Rouletabille.

---

**SIGHTS NEARBY**

Opposite Jellinek's tomb, turn left to see that of Gastaud, which is supported from below by its occupant's two hands …

## HÔTEL WINDSOR

11, rue Dalpozzo • Tel: 04 93 88 59 35 • www.hotelwindsornice.com
• E-mail: contact@hotelwindsornice.com
• Room rates from €80 to €165

> *When the bedrooms are all unique works of art ...*

The rooms of the Windsor Hotel Parmigianni, each a unique work of art, were designed by different artists who could create a complete functional space. Thus Parmigianni conceived of a golden cube with a stripped-down white bed. This is the journalists' favourite room in that it is the most spectacular. The bedroom created by Ben, or that by Joël Ducorroy, are striking for their humorous references. Palestine Charlemagne, Jean-Pierre Bertrand, Philippe Perrin, François Morelet, Glenn Baxter and many others have also given free rein to their imaginations. Room 238, designed by Varini, has something special: the red line that crosses the room, entrance hall and bathroom is only visible from a single well-defined point. Allow some time to explore the room to find out where …

---

### OTHER UNUSUAL (BUT NOT ALWAYS SECRET) HOTELS AND BARS IN NICE

#### ROOMS WITH A VIEW: HÔTEL ACANTHE

2, rue Chauvain • Tel: 04 93 62 22 44 • www.hotel-acanthe-nice.cote.azur.fr
• Rotunda room rates €53 to €61 according to season. Breakfast €4

In the very heart of the town, the Acanthe is a one-star hotel with a sharp angle that makes the building very narrow where it comes to a point: this corner, laid out as a rotunda, is home to four original rooms offering an exceptional panorama of the city. A quality/price ratio difficult to beat in Nice.

#### HI-HÔTEL (photo lower right)

3, avenue des Fleurs • Tel: 04 97 07 26 26 • www.hi-hotel.net
• Romm rates: €145 to €350 per night.

Designed by Matali Crasset, former collaborator of Philippe Starck, Hi-Hôtel (thirty-eight rooms) has become a design landmark on the Côte d'Azur. Its restaurant is a fashionable venue in Nice.

#### LE WATER BAR

10, rue de la Loge • Tel: 04 93 62 56 50
• Open 18.00–0.30 in winter and 12.00–0.30 in summer. Closed Monday.

In the same style as Colette in Paris, the Water Bar offers an extremely wide range of mineral waters from around the world.

#### BRASSERIE FLO

4, rue Sacha-Guitry • Tel: 04 93 13 38 38 • www.flonice.com
• Set meals from €18.90 to €28.90.

Although it has a spectacular dining room on the ground floor of Nice's former *caf'conc'* [café-concert, with live music] and forms part of the celebrated Brasserie Flo group, the Nice branch strangely enough does not appear in many of the guides to the region. Inaugurated in 1897 and later becoming a casino under the Folies Bergères banner, the cooking offered is unfortunately the chain standard, that is, relatively nondescript.

## THE BUSSOPHONE OF LOUIS-NUCERA LIBRARY

Bibliothèque Louis-Nucera
2, place Yves-Klein • Tel: 04 97 13 48 00
• E-mail : info@bmvr-nice.com • www.bmvr-nice.com.fr
• Open Tuesday and Wednesday 10.00–19.00; Thursday and Friday
14.00–19.00; Saturday 10.00–18.00 • July and August from Tuesday to
Saturday 13.00–18.00

> ### *Cousin of the jukebox*

The architecture of the offices of the municipal library for the Nice region is very much out of the ordinary. Installed in the "square head" of Sacha Sosno – a cube on top of a "human" neck of gigantic proportions. Nearby is the bibliothèque Louis-Nucera, the town's main reference library.

In the discothèque section is a historic machine called the *bussophone*. Invented in 1920 and electrified in 1932, this cousin of the jukebox was the brainchild of Michel Bussoz (1872–1958), whence the name. The original model, taking twenty 78 records at a time, was certainly automatic but worked by mechanical "propulsion". You played a record by inserting a token (*jeton Bussoz*), marked "25 centimes to use" (or 30 with inflation). Now collectors' items, these tokens are also marked with a heart or trefoil.

Photo Stéphane Bidault - www.jetons-monnaie.net

---

### THE JUKEBOX

The first working jukebox was installed at San Francisco in 1889 by Louis Glass and his associate William S. Arnold. It was already a coin-operated phonograph that earned them over $1,000 in its first six months. But it was the Wurlitzer family who would fully develop the concept with the P10 model, gaining 60% of the American market. After the Second World War, the market exploded in Europe with the simultaneous arrival of Stateside music. Between 1946 and 1947, Wurlitzer would sell more than 56,000 machines worldwide.

## SOCIÉTÉ GÉNÉRALE HEADQUARTERS, NICE ⓬

8, avenue Jean-Médecin

*Robbery of the century*

An imposing building located just at the beginning of avenue Jean-Médecin, next to place Masséna, the headquarters of the Société Générale bank is well-known for having been the target of what has long been called the "robbery of the century".

Albert Spaggiari, the brains behind this unprecedented heist, got the idea from a detective novel by Robert Pollock, *Tous à l'égout*, and stopped at nothing in his desire to turn fiction into fact. Finding the sewer leading under the bank demanded days of scouting around the entrails of Nice. Then he had to recruit a team of specialists and finally, make a superhuman effort to move around in these tunnels filled with rubbish and rats, carrying equipment and digging a tunnel 8 metres long that came out in the bank strongroom. Over the weekend of 17–18 July 1976, the team got through and began to blow up the safe doors. They found gold ingots and sovereigns, *objets d'art*, pornographic photographs, compromising documents and, the cherry on the cake, sacks stuffed with banknotes everywhere (cash deposited for the weekend by the bank's shopkeeper clients). Caught unawares by the rising water in the sewers, the criminals had to cut short their efforts and make their escape.

They "only" opened 317 safe boxes out of the 4,100 in the strongroom, and their loot was calculated at over 50 million old francs. The police would find no trace other than their abandoned equipment, cooking utensils and canteen, with these words on a slip of paper stuck to a safe: *Sans arme, sans violence et sans haine* [No arms, no violence and no hate].

Albert Spaggiari was eventually arrested by the police, but managed to flee through the window of the judge's office on the first floor of the law courts. On the run for the rest of his life, he died in 1989 suffering from cancer, aged 57.

### SIGHTS NEARBY

#### THE MORABITO BUILDING – NO ENTRANCE ⓭
13, avenue Jean-Médecin

Opposite the Société Générale, a sharply-angled building is scarcely noticeable unless you stand where you can see the meeting of its two façades. It seems to have no entrance: access is in fact by a stairway in the ground-floor café, although you can also get to one of the floors via the neighbouring building. The work of the architect Guilgot, this elegant and strange building was constructed in 1953.

## THE ISBA OF VALROSE PARK

Science Faculty
Parc Valrose
• Officially, access to the faculty is limited to students and you have to get
permission to enter the park and view the isba (from the outside only): check
with the faculty administration at least a month in advance at the address
above, or by e-mail: direction-sciences@unice.fr.

> **An traditional Russian house on campus**

Classified as a historic monument in 1991, the authentic isba in Valrose Park can be found by going into the campus of the science faculty by the majestic entrance on boulevard Prince-de-Galles (take the small stairway and the rock-garden underpass that leads down and then go left to the natural sciences building. The isba is just behind).

It's an intriguing tale: a modest piano teacher, Baron Von Derwies was introduced to stocks and shares by one of his pupils. His rise was spectacular. Banker and owner of railway tracks (the future trans-Siberian line), he amassed a considerable fortune. In 1866, at the age of 45, he decided to retire from business to concentrate on his private life … At this time he bought the Valrose estate where he had a chateau built together with park and imitation ruins, devoting himself to his great passion, music.

The isba, "high note" of his domain, was dismantled from one of the baron's properties near Kiev, in Ukraine. The pinewood building and its slate roof were transported in sections by river and sea and reconstructed in the park with all its original fittings, from door handle to nails. On some friezes there are proverbs: *Bière n'est point nectar, hydromel point ambroisie quand l'amour en douceur les surpasse* … [Beer is not nectar at all, nor hydromel ambrosia, when sweet love transcends them …]. Was this what the baron was thinking he showed his female round the isba?

Only the exterior of the building, which used to be a teachers' home, can now be visited.

---

### THE MIDDAY CANNON

Since 1860, every day at 12 noon precisely, the cannon roars in Nice. The initiative came from Sir Thomas Coventry More, a Scottish resident who in this way let his wife, who tended to be slow getting lunch, know what time it was. In fact it is a pyrotechnist who from the heights of the chateau sets off a rocket, that classic firework that just makes a loud noise.

Although all the locals are obviously aware of this, many tourists are taken aback when it happens …

## THE FIRST COASTAL MOTOR RACE IN THE WORLD ⓯
Boulevard Bischoffsheim

> *The deadly bend of the Grande Corniche*

Right at the start of the Grande Corniche route, boulevard Bischoffsheim (named after the founder of the Nice Observatory located on this road), on the left going up, a commemorative stone marker recalls here the racing cars set off to compete in the first coastal run between Nice and La Turbie

This motor race was first staged on 31 July 1897 and won by André Michelin in the car category, driving a steam car with pneumatic tyres made by …. Michelin. Six three-wheelers from Dion Bouton finished among the first seven of the motorcycle category.

A few metres further along, just after the first bend, on the right side of boulevard Bischoffsheim, there are plaques to the memory of two victims of the first bend of the track. They are Wilhem Bauer, mortally injured on 30 March 1900 at the wheel of a Daimler Phoenix, watched by Emil Jellinek (see page 59), who used the accident as an argument to ask Daimler to improve the road-holding qualities of their cars. The other plaque pays homage to Elliott Zborowski who died tragically on 1 April 1903.

## ANSALDI'S BIRTHPLACE

31, boulevard Riquier

> *The real life of HRH Prince Louis-Eugène Alexandre d'Ansaldi*

At the corner of boulevard Riquier and boulevard Delfino, at number 31 boulevard Riquier, a plaque on the left gatepost is easy to miss. Ivy partly covers it and the inscription is wearing away. But you can still make out: "Ansaldi was born in this house on 6 April 1908".

Enquiries as to the identify of this Ansaldi are difficult, and for good reason: he invented his entire princely biography ... which let him pull off a few fine hoaxes abroad as well as in France.

The life story that he had thought up for himself saw him descended from King Victor-Emmanuel II of Italy, and a certain Madame Ansaldi, a beautiful Niçoise woman, who supposedly became pregnant after a brief royal encounter ... Clearly not wanting to recognize the child, the king ennobled the woman's husband by way of compensation. In this way the Ansaldi on the plaque claimed to be grandson of HRH Prince André d'Ansaldi and son of HRH Prince Benoît.

The man himself, known as HRH Prince Louis-Eugène Alexandre d'Ansaldi, set up a foundation in his name, the Œuvre Nationale du Théâtre à l'Hôpital, a simple association of friends that would later become the Académie Ansaldi in Paris, an international institution founded in 1933, recognized as a public service and honoured with an award by the President of the Republic in 1947.

Thanks to this fictional fame, Ansaldi managed to have streets named after him, in several countries! He published documents flattering himself and had stamps issued bearing his image.

As for the plaque on the boulevard Riquier, it was naturally Ansaldi who put it there.

# THE SERAPHIC CROSS OF CIMIEZ*

Place du monastère de Cimiez

*A unique
image*

In the square of Cimiez monastery, now laid out as a parking space for visitors to the monastery, a column of false marble is surmounted by a crucifix. Observant visitors will notice that this Christ doesn't quite conform to traditional iconography: it is in fact a crucified seraph (see box), represented according to the vision of St Francis of Assisi in his cell on Mount Alverno, Tuscany, as he received the stigmata of Christ's Passion. It is thus no coincidence that this monument was formerly in the first Franciscan convent built in 1250 in the old city of Nice, place Saint-François.

St Francis is moreover shown to the right of the cross, with St Louis of Toulouse to the left. On top, a pelican regurgitating its food to nourish its young symbolizes Christ's sacrifice to save mankind. Finally, at the foot of the cross, are the arms of the Sardina family (three sardines) who took part in the restoration of the monument in 1804: in 1793, during the Revolution, the cross had been broken up and someone collected and hid the fragments until the Concordat of 1801.

This cross, as the inscription indicates, was carved in 1477 on the orders of the Franciscan brother Louis Terrini to watch over the cemetery of the congregation. Following an act of vandalism in 1979, the original cross is now inside the church in the first side chapel on the left. The one standing outside is just a replica.

(*) According to the heritage service of the Ville de Nice. The other image of a seraph on the cross is in the chapel of Villaret at Montgirod (Savoie). Surmounting a retable dating from 1673, it is attributed to Gualla. It shows a bearded, long-haired figure with three pairs of wings in place of limbs. To find out more: www.sabaudia.org/v2/dossiers/baroque/18.htm

## ANGELS, ARCHANGELS AND SERAPHIM

Angels are the messengers of God. The Catholic hierarchy of angels has nine orders or angelic choirs which are, from highest to lowest ranking: seraphim, cherubim, thrones, dominions, virtues, powers, principalities, archangels and finally angels. This "hierarchy" is not really divisive as the separation between the nine angelic choirs is closely related to their different functions. In the Bible, the seraphim (Hebrew for "burning ones") are described by Isaiah as having three pairs of wings: one for concealing their faces, one for flying and one to spread over their feet. They surround the throne of God and sing His praises. They also have the power to raise up lesser beings and are known as the "burners" of sin. Each seraph is concerned with one of the seven mortal sins which he can help us to overcome.

The archangels, according to the Bible, are seven in number. Three are officially recognized: Michael (he who saw off the demon in the Apocalypse), Raphael (sent by God to cure the blindness of Tobias' father and help him to meet Sarah, thus securing the line of Abraham; it was also he who revealed to Tobias the existence of seven archangels) and Gabriel (who announced to Mary that she would be mother of the Son of God).

## THE ABBEY OF SAINT-PONS

Chemin de l'Abbaye-de-Saint-Pons
Church open during the day

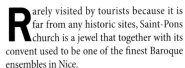

> *Hemmed in behind the Pasteur Hospital, Saint-Pons church has been gradually forgotten ...*

**R**arely visited by tourists because it is far from any historic sites, Saint-Pons church is a jewel that together with its convent used to be one of the finest Baroque ensembles in Nice.

Pons, a Roman prefect, was converted to Christianity and took refuge at Cemenelum* when the emperor Valerian launched a vast wave of persecution of the Christians. He was beheaded there around AD 253. The saint's relics are preserved in the church and presented to followers on his feast day, 14 May.

Founded in the 8th century, Saint-Pons abbey enjoyed wide influence in the region during the Middle Ages. It owned the site of the present old town of Nice and founded churches further inland. The abbey's decline began in the 16th century and the construction in three stages of the Pasteur hospital in the 20th century tend to marginalize the church, its convent buildings having been taken over by the psychiatric services of the hospital.

The church, reconstructed in 1724, is now missing one of its two original symmetrical belltowers. The major point of interest of the façade is a covered courtyard beyond a row of arches, above which a terrace gave access to the convent.

Inside, you will find the curved spaces typical of Baroque churches in and around Nice.

(*) Cemenelum was the Latin name for Cimiez, a Roman town now part of the Nice conglomeration. You can visit a number of ruins of which the best-known are the arenas and a remarkable museum.

### SIGHTS NEARBY

#### THE WANDERING WAR MEMORIAL OF CIMIEZ

Also in the monastery square is the memorial to the fallen soldiers of Cimiez, consisting of a marble stele and a bronze sculpture by Michel de Tarnowsky (1870–1946). A metre high and weighing some 300 kilos, it represents a broken broadsword and a helmet topped by the Gallic cock laying low the Prussian eagle. The survival of this bronze today is a near miracle: in 1940, the sculpture was immersed in the sea out of sight of the occupying forces, who wanted to melt it down to recuperate the metal as well as destroying an image that reflected badly on them. It was replaced after the war, but in 1989 it was stolen and offered for sale in the flea market in cours Saleya, right in the city centre. It was the mayor of Nice himself who, strolling through the market, recognized it and arranged for it to be restored to the city. The original work is now preserved in a safe place and, in the monastery square, like the seraph's cross, is a copy that you can muse over ...

(Source: *Lou Sourgentin* magazine, number 122)

# THE RUSSIAN CEMETERY

Avenue Sainte-Marguerite • Tel: 04 93 83 94 08
• Open Tuesday 14.00–17.00, Wednesday and Thursday 9.00–12.00 and 14.00–
17.00, Friday and Saturday 9.00–12.00 and 14.00–18.00, Sunday 14.00–18.00
• Access: avenue Sainte-Marguerite opens into place Caucade, where the
entrance to the cemetery is located. Leave your vehicle in the vicinity. Walk
through the impasse opposite marked by a small sign: "Cimetière russe".

> **The tomb
> of Katia, mistress
> of Tsar Alexander II**

Located on a gentle slope overlooking the sea, the Russian cemetery in Nice is a magnificent place where only the planes flying in and out of France's second airport disturbs the serene atmosphere. The couple of guardians that have recently arrived have not yet completely mastered the French language, but with good grace they will show you a historic document as well as a detailed plan to help you find the tomb of Princess Catherine Yourevski. Better known as Katia, her life has inspired several novels, such as *Katia, le démon bleu du Tsar Alexandre* by Princess Bibesco, adapted for the cinema in 1959 by Robert Siodmak with Romy Schneider and Curd Jürgens in the principal roles.

Tsar Alexander II fell for this poverty-stricken young woman during a visit to a school for children of fallen nobility. But rumours of their clandestine passion spread and the tsar agreed that Katia should be kept away from him. But he found her again in France during a state visit to Napoleon III and she thus became his official mistress. Worn out by illness and heartbroken, the empress died and Alexander was free to marry Katia. Not long afterwards the tsar was the victim of an assassination attempt and died in the arms of his morganatic spouse.*

The princess then left Russia where she had lived since her marriage and settled in Nice, in Villa Georges (now demolished), boulevard Dubouchage. She also spent time at Château Valrose and the isba of her friend Paul Georgevitch Von Derwies (see article on the isba of Château Valrose, page 65).

(*) A "morganatic" marriage is that of a woman who has married a man of higher birth or rank and who cannot claim to succeed to his hereditary titles and property.

## THE RUSSIAN PRESENCE IN NICE

In the 19th century, the Russian aristocracy would choose Nice as their winter residence. The craze for sea-bathing in the summer finally sealed the city's reputation and made it the favoured resort of the Russian nobility and all those who had the means of escaping the northern snows or to come for a TB cure in the good sea air. The first Russian Orthodox chapel in rue Longchamp soon proved too cramped and in 1905 construction began of St Nicolas Cathedral, completed in 1912. Finally, the 1917 Revolution would precipitate the exile of White Russians, many of whom settled in Nice.

# AROUND NICE

# THE STONE OF COURSEGOULES

Mairie de Coursegoules
• 1, place de la Mairie 06140 Coursegoules
• Open during office hours

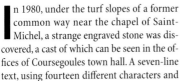

*Mysterious writing*

I n 1980, under the turf slopes of a former common way near the chapel of Saint-Michel, a strange engraved stone was discovered, a cast of which can be seen in the offices of Coursegoules town hall. A seven-line text, using fourteen different characters and apparently incomplete, is carved on it. Although certain similarities with the Greek alphabet and Punic (Carthaginian) writing are recognizable, the language is unknown. The mystery was taken seriously but remained unsolved, despite research by epigraphists from the French Centre National de la Recherche Scientifique, the École Pratique des Hautes Études (Sorbonne) and the Académie des Inscriptions et Belles-Lettres (Institut de France). If some have found this writing "interesting", others have cast doubt on its authenticity, dismissing it as "fanciful"!

**SIGHTS NEARBY**

### FORMER FREINET SCHOOL

35, rue de l'Escaou
06140 Coursegoules

The strange façade of the Freinet school at Coursegoules was designed by the pupils.
For further information on the Freinet method see section on Le Bar-sur-Loup, page 171.

# EX-VOTO TO THE FLU

Chemin des Granges
06140 Coursegoules

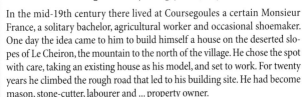

> *A moving testimony to the influenza epidemic*

**A**fter crossing the bridge over the Cagne river, at right angles to the first right turn, chemin des Granges leads after some 30 m to a retaining wall blocking the way. This wall is home to a strange ex-voto, probably brought here as stone recuperated from another site, which apparently gives thanks for escaping the 1837 flu epidemic. This epidemic, which appeared in 1832, would spread throughout Europe and leave at least 100,000 dead.

The most deadly flu epidemic in history was the Spanish influenza of 1918, responsible for 40 million deaths, a figure far beyond the Asian flu of 1957 (4 million deaths) and the Hong Kong flu in 1968 (2 million deaths).

**SIGHTS NEARBY**

### THE HOUSE OF THE HANGED MAN

Montagne du Cheiron 06140 Coursegoules
• Access: from the village, take the path signposted chapel of Saint-Michel

In the mid-19th century there lived at Coursegoules a certain Monsieur France, a solitary bachelor, agricultural worker and occasional shoemaker. One day the idea came to him to build himself a house on the deserted slopes of Le Cheiron, the mountain to the north of the village. He chose the spot with care, taking an existing house as his model, and set to work. For twenty years he climbed the rough road that led to his building site. He had become mason, stone-cutter, labourer and ... property owner.

Once the house was finished, he began to build the *restanques* (dry-stone terracing) – so sturdily that they are still standing today and clearly visible from the village. His titanic labour complete, Monsieur France decided to climb to the top of the mountain to admire his work. And there, facing the symbol of his solitude, surrounded by the arid slopes of Le Cheiron, he understood that it had all been in vain. So he went home, took a rope, and hanged himself on the lime tree he had planted there twenty years earlier.

# THE PASSION CROSS

Rue Torrin-et-Grassi
06510 Gattières

*A rare
example of the
Passion Cross*

A Passion Cross shows the instruments used to torture and execute Christ, as well as the crucifix itself. Dating from 1806, that of Gattières, one of the latest to be found in the Côte d'Azur, is made from wrought iron. Placed on top of a stone column, this trefoil cross shows the chalice that collected Christ's blood (that would become the Holy Grail), the spear used to check that He was dead, the ladder to raise Him up onto the Cross and then to take Him down again, the sponge soaked in gall and vinegar, two rods used for the flogging, the hammer to enter the nails, three nails, the pincers to pull out the nails, the crown of thorns and, finally, the sign "INRI", standing for "Jesus of Nazareth, King of the Jews".

Although missing from Gattières, other instruments can sometimes be found on Passion Crosses: Malchus' lantern, which identified Christ in the Garden of Gethsemane, the sword with which Peter cut off Malchus' ear, the ewer recalling Pontius Pilate's washing of hands, the heart, symbolic of Christ's love to save mankind, the dice used by the soldiers gambling for Christ's tunic, the sun, recalling that the sun was covered at the death of Christ, and finally the cock that evokes the three denials of the apostle Peter.

Sought after for their value in the art market, the wrought-iron crosses are rare and often replaced by cast-iron ones. Also, by the way, the small wooden cross that gave its name to the Croisette at Cannes no longer exists …

**MALCHUS**

Servant of the high priest Caiaphas, Malchus was about to arrest Jesus in the Garden of Gethsemane when Peter cut off his right ear with a sword. Jesus immediately healed him.

# THE HOLE IN THE STONE

Route du Clot-de-Dué 06670 Saint-Martin-du-Var
• Access: from the village of Saint-Martin-du-Var, take the RN202 in the direction of Nice and turn left towards the Condamines and the Saint-Joseph district. Continue along the Condamines road for 1.7 km. Turn left onto Route des Maquisards for 1.4 km. At the crossroads, turn left along Route de la Croix-de-Claud for 60 m. Turn right onto Route du Clot-de-Dué. At the junction you'll find the stone.

*A mysterious megalith*

**S**tanding at the side of the road, an odd-looking stone measuring just over a metre high by some 40 cm wide is pierced by a perfectly cylindrical hole 20 cm in diameter. It is known as the *pierre trouée* [holed stone] or *peire pertuaù* in *Nissart*. There is no known explanation for this..

### SIGHTS NEARBY

### ALLEGORY OF PEACE
Square Léo-Mauran 06670 Saint-Martin-du-Var

In 1957, the municipality of Saint-Martin-du-Var commissioned an allegory of peace from Roland Brice, pupil of Fernand Léger. Composed of a ceramic wall panel and a mosaic basin, the work is really out of place today in this well-ordered village. It shows a child's face and a dove realized in Fernand Léger's habitual colours.

### SIGN OF THE BLACKSMITH VET **8**
Place de la Forge 06910 Roquesteron
Visits by appointment from
Monsieur Gilles Passeron-Seybald • Tel: 04 93 05 94 60 or 06 80 14 02 19
M. Alain Dalmasso • Tel: 06 80 30 57 30 • E-mail: alain02.dalmasso@wanadoo.fr
*Alziary Napoléon maréchal-ferrant vétérinaire praticien* [Alziary Napoléon blacksmith-farrier practising veterinary surgeon]. This marvellous sign, now restored, was that of the blacksmith-farrier of the village of Roquesteron. Having set up his forge at this address in 1798, he obtained a certificate allowing him to practise the trade of veterinary surgeon. Inside, a collection of blacksmith's tools and instruments, such as bellows and hammers, have been preserved. In 1917, for safety reasons, the forge moved to the outskirts of the village. The Association du Four à Pain et du Pressoir (see contact details above) tries to preserve the village heritage and offers free guided visits to the forge, the bread oven, the wine press, the former butcher's shop, the oil mill and the the shoemaker's shop.

### THE CIPPE (*) OF ROQUESTERON **9**
Rue de la Voie-Romaine 06910 Roquesteron

Set into the stone filling of a wall in rue de la Voie-Romaine, a funerary slab a metre tall carries the ensignia of a centurion (Roman military commander of 100 soldiers) and of a decurion (10 soldiers), as well as a dagger and crescent.

(*) A *cippe* is a funerary monument indicating the presence of a tomb and carrying an inscription.

# MUSÉE DES MÉTIERS D'AUTREFOIS

3250, route de Gilette 06830 Gilette
• Tel: 04 92 08 96 04 and 06 80 45 12 08
• Open from May to September 9.00–19.00, October to April 10.00–17.30
Admission: €4

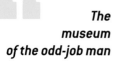

**The museum of the odd-job man**

Set up by Pierre-Guy Martelly, who gives regular demonstrations there of the blacksmith's trade, the astonishing museum of bygone trades presents the tools and instruments of now disappeared professions.

Depending on the objects on display, visitors' reactions can be very different: the tools of yesterday's dentist, for example, a real collection of instruments of torture, will let some people appreciate the undeniable progress of dental surgery or freeze the blood of the most sensitive souls.

In a very interesting way, the museum's founder has also recreated workshops using authentic tools and machinery, as for example the vehicle repair shop. Some pieces from Auguste Maïcon's aircraft are also exhibited. Explanatory panels and photographs tell the story of this aviation pioneer beloved of Côte d'Azur residents. And for good reason: on 24 August 1919, he succeeded in the exploit of flying below the arch of the Pont du Var, 6 m high, in his 4 m high plane …

Better still, turning the craft, Maïcon repeated his performance. From then on he was known as the *Lindbergh niçois* [Lindbergh of Nice]. At the time, the exploit, filmed and photographed, attracted a lot of attention and pictures of it are to be seen in the museum.

Naturally, a plane resting on a sloping meadow indicates to passers-by the entrance to this not to be missed museum.

# THE "BOUTAU" STONE

Place de la Liberté
06670 Levens

> *"We're jumping on Grimaldi's belly!"*

Marked by an explanatory panel, a strange stone emerges from the ground, place de la Liberté. Once you've read it you'll understand how the square got its name …

At the beginning of the 17th century, Annibal Grimaldi, governor of Nice, was suspected of treason towards the duchy of Savoy. After various incidents, he was condemned for the crimes of lese-majesty, rebellion and felony, and condemned to death in absentia. Holed up in his chateau, Tourrettes-Revest, he was to be strangled by the Savoyard forces.

The residents of Levens, who were closely following these events, at this point staged an uprising. Their lord and master, César Grimaldi, cousin of Annibal, afraid of suffering the same fate as his relative, left to find shelter in his chateau at Cabris. The people of Levens seized the opportunity to take over the chateau in Levens itself, demolish it and thus declare themselves a free commune. The commune was even recognized by the Duke of Savoy, Charles-Emmanuel, who granted Levens the title *comtesse d'elle-même* [countess, i.e. mistress, of her own destiny].

To mark their victory, the people of Levens were to install this stone, known as the "Boutau" (literally the stone you jump on) and personalize it in the shape of the virtual belly of César Grimaldi. Today they still commemorate this event during their feast day (2 September) by jumping on the stone shouting, "We're jumping on Grimaldi's belly!" This custom is of course scarcely appreciated in Monaco …

## SIGHTS NEARBY

### THE DONKEY'S RING
10, avenue Docteur-Faraut
06670 Levens

A short distance from esplanade Louis-Roux, avenue Docteur-Faraut leads to place de la République, the centre of village life. Immediately to the left, an eye-catching door with a decorated lintel is dedicated to the cleric who lived in this house, the *Maioun dou Padre* [Father's House]. At the side of the door, a solitary iron ring embedded in the wall is surmounted by a pretty enamelled tile representing a donkey and bearing the inscription *Càu estacà doun voi lou mestre* [tie up the donkey where the master wants it]. Note that the Levens dialect is known as Levenssois and differs from *Nissart* in its Alpine (*gavotte*) influences.

# THE PAINTING *L'ENFER ET LE PARADIS*
## IN THE CHAPEL OF THE PÉNITENTS-BLANCS

06420 La Tour
Ask for key at the town hall
An audio commentary to the visit is available

> *Those risen from the dead leave their tombs*

**D**ecorated in 1491 by the Nice painters Nadal and Brevesi, the chapel of the Pénitents-Blancs in La Tour is a must for lovers of the unusual and unexpected. Although the side walls show scenes from the Passion of Christ and the ceiling the evangelists, the decoration of the chevet [apse behind high altar] is the most spectacular feature: a retable bordered by two scenes of the Last Judgement: Hell and Heaven, above which those risen from the dead can be seen leaving their tombs.

To the left, Saint Peter fits his key in the lock to open the door of the heavenly Jerusalem to the men and women waiting on a staircase as naked as the day they were born. An angel guides them to their fate.

The lock of the chapel itself is by the way decorated with two penitents …

To the right, dragons, monsters, leviathans and all kinds of demons prepare the damned on earth for the torments of Hell. Their bodies are already criss-crossed with red from the whips of their tormentors. The entrance to Hell is represented by the head of a monster (probably a leviathan) in which those not yet entirely conscious of the (awful) fate awaiting them are swallowed up.

---

### LEVIATHAN

Leviathan (from the Hebrew *Livyatan*) is a sea monster mentioned in the Bible's Book of Job, whose name evokes a colossal beast. Some sources cite its name as one of the principal demons of Hell. In the Middle Ages, it was often represented as a gaping maw that swallowed souls.

---

### SIGHTS NEARBY

### THE KULACINSKI HOUSE
Grand Place 06420 La Tour

Named after its new owners, the Kulacinski house is a former hospital of the Holy Sepulchre with a remarkable *trompe l'oeil* painted façade. Although the building itself dates back to the 15th century, this decoration seems to have been carried out during the presidential mandate of Sadi Carnot (1887–94), whose painted bust is on the first floor.

Under the arches on which the house is built, you can see a frieze dating from the 18th century and illustrating the articles sold at the time when the ground floor harboured a grocer's cum haberdasher's bazaar. Household goods and tableware, pottery and pewterware, are also represented.

Finally, on the right wall of the arches is a Greek inscription which translates as "Alas, one must die".

## THE PENITENTS

In Provence and the Côte d'Azur, a great many chapels bear witness to the social importance of the brotherhoods of penitents before the Revolution. Appearing at the beginning of the13th century, the penitents seemed to owe their existence to the Roman Catholic Church's proclamation of the end of public penances (mainly processions of flagellants): those who wanted to take upon themselves the sins of others.

Their mission consisted above all in relieving the anguish of prisoners condemned to death or in gathering up the dead from the public highway. It sometimes happened that different brotherhoods ended up fighting over an inert body, like competitors for clients. Note that if the victim was not a pauper, they charged burial fees.

The various brotherhoods were differentiated by the colour of their robes (which also served as funeral shrouds). The first to set up in a town chose white and this took precedence over other colours, notably during processions where white robes headed the cortege. Next came the black penitents who were most often in charge of collecting the dead who had no family from the streets, organizing paupers' funerals and moral support for those condemned to death. The remaining brotherhoods choice of colour had no particular significance: thus there were blue, red or grey penitents who all carried out the same social services.

The penitents were also said to respect the rule of anonymity, as borne out by the hood they wore through which only their eyes could be glimpsed. Finally, the last common feature was their rope, symbolizing exaltation and discipline.

Banned in 1792, the brotherhoods would often infiltrate freemasonry. Today, certain groups have reformed themselves, mainly in the large towns (Nice for example) and are very active. Processions take place in Holy Week, during which their rattles announce services in place of the church bells, silent at that time.

Finally, at Gorbio, for the feast of the Holy Sacrament or Fête-Dieu, the "snail procession" sees the penitents of different brotherhoods gather to traverse the village lit only by snail shells in which oil-soaked wicks burn.

To find out more: Maurice Aghulon, *Pénitents et francs-maçons de l'ancienne Provence*, ÉditionsFayard.

## THE TITHING TROUGH

Rue du Four 06260 Puget-Rostang

**15**

Indicated a the sign in rue du Four, without which it would probably have gone unnoticed, is an remarkable tithing trough, used under the ancien régime to measure la *dîme* (the tithe), the contribution in kind to the clergy's expenses.

*A reminder of the tithe*

### LA *DÎME*

Payment of la *dîme*, as tithes were called in France, became a religious obligation in AD 585 and mandatory under Charlemagne (AD 794). Affecting all landowners and varying between an eleventh and a thirteenth part of agricultural produce and livestock, the tithe was turned over to the ecclesiastical authorities so that the Church could support parish priests, maintain religious buildings and hospitals and offer poor relief. The part given to priests was known as the *portion congrue* [smallest share]. The revolutionaries abolished the tithe on 4 August 1789 at the same time as other privileges enjoyed by the French aristocracy under the Ancien Régime.

### SIGHTS NEARBY

A VISION OF THE VIRGIN IN THE ALPES-MARITIMES?
**NOTRE-DAME-DE-LA-ROUDOULE**
502, route de la Roudoule 06260 Puget-Théniers

**16**

On the road from Puget-Théniers to Puget-Rostang, a shrine catches the eye. Notre-Dame-de-la-Roudoule, also known as the oratory of Notre-Dame-de-Lourdes, was built on the very spot where apparitions of the Virgin occurred at the beginning of the 20th century. On Saturday 20 May 1916, Jeanne Martin and Adeline Biehler, two little girls aged 7 and 11, were herding goats when they are said to have glimpsed a "White Lady" surrounded by a luminous halo. This "White Lady" is also said to have revealed details of soldiers who had been missing for some time, telling the girls that news of the men would be coming soon. And, strangely, so it came to pass. The girls' story was nevertheless doubted, but … miracles and prayers for protection unfailingly comforted those who believed in them.

# THE HIDDEN BUST OF ABBOT JEAN-PIERRE PAPON

14, rue Papon
06260 Puget-Théniers

> *A very special abbot*

The bust of Abbot Jean-Pierre Papon, 7 m high, between the second and third floor of the house where he was born, is so well hidden from passers-by that many of the residents of Puget-Théniers don't know of its existence. You need a pair of binoculars or a telephoto lens to see any details of this sculpture, which was installed in the 19th century.

Born in 1734 in this very house, Jean-Pierre Papon studied philosophy and literature. But it was his nomination to run the Marseilles library that would decide his life's work: to write the history of Provence and the region that would later be known as the Côte d'Azur, because for our abbot, Provence stretched from Nice to Sisteron, Marseille to Digne and Fréjus to Avignon …

If today his four-volume *Histoire générale de la Provence* is rarely consulted, his *Voyage en Provence* (published by La Découverte) is still an essential guide to the region. Written in a style both clear and graphic, the book has the huge merit of never falling into cliché or stilted language. Nothing was allowed to escape the learned Papon, from the ugliness of such and such a town to criticism of its residents, from the rigours of the climate to memories of catastrophes. He made constructive comments, suggesting here to enlarge a canal, there to widen a street. His erudition and curiosity meant that he could evoke the Roman period while describing mineral riches, animal species or local plants. A *bon vivant*, the gourmet abbot never forgot any dish or wine in the towns and villages he visited. But it is especially his feeling for anecdote and unusual detail that makes his work so interesting, witty and humorous, not something that can be said of all scholars.

## SIGHTS NEARBY

A boundary stone that indicated the border between the County of Nice and France has been moved in front of the tourist office. It was formerly on the line that followed the river. On one side it bears the cross of Savoy (Nice was part of the house of Savoy until 1860) and on the other, the *fleur de lys*, emblem of the kingdom of France.

At number 4 rue Papon the stones above the door bear a mitre and cross, the sole vestiges of the former Augustine convent, and the insignia of the prior, whose unseemly behaviour led to the closure of the convent shortly before the Revolution.

# FORMER SKI-JUMP AT BEUIL

Quartier La Condamine 06470 Beuil-les-Launes

> *Evidence of the introduction of Nordic skiing in the Alpes-Maritimes*

Although the first skiing competition in Alpes-Maritimes took place at Peïra-Cava in 1909, it was only after the First World War that mountain resorts grew up offering winter sports facilities. It was largely thanks to *chevalier* Victor de Cessole, photographer, humanist, scholar and mountain-lover, that the Beuil site was developed and equipped with a ski-jump that can still be seen today. It was opened in 1930, during a competition in which Marcel Payot, French ski-jump champion at the time, was taking part.

Nordic skiing brings together all the Scandinavian-influenced disciplines: cross-country, jumps, Alpine/Nordic combination and biathlon.

## SIGHTS NEARBY

### THE PRESIDENTS' GALLERY (photos above and lower left)

Hôtel de Ville • 4300, avenue du Général-de-Gaulle 06710 Touët-sur-Var
• Open Monday, Tuesday, Thursday, Friday 9.00–12.00 and 14.00–16.00;
Wednesday and Saturday 9.00–12.00 • Admission free

Despite its obvious assets (a fine perched village, the famous Pignes train and an exceptional rural environment), Touët-sur-Var has not managed to make itself known. One day the idea was broached of creating a portrait gallery of the 22 successive Presidents of the Republic until 1997. In that year, the commune purely and simply won the marvellous Marianne d'Or prize for this initiative. Each official portrait is presented with a biography and an accompanying booklet is on sale for €6.50.

### TORRENT UNDER THE AISLE OF THE PARISH CHURCH (photo lower right)

Le Planet • Avenue Désiré-Niel 06710 Touët-sur-Var

In the perched village (sometimes called the "Tibetan village"), on the floor of the central aisle of the church, a wooden trapdoor can be raised to offer a dizzying view down to the ravine over which the building was constructed. The torrent flows beneath your feet in a most unexpected way.

### MARIANNE D'OR

The Marianne d'Or is the top French municipal award. The competition rewards communes throughout France for notable initiatives. The prize was set up in 1984 by parliamentarian Edgar Faure and Alain Trampogliéri, a former journalist and Saint-Tropez town councillor at the time. The award, in the form of a golden bust by the celebrated jeweller Cartier, is presented in a red and gold casket.

# THE BOAR OF ILONSE

Mairie d'Ilonse
Place Serret
06420 Ilonse
• Tel: 04 93 02 03 49

I n 1998, a rare Gallic bronze boar dating from the first century BC was found in the Loirins district of Ilonse, a most beautiful isolated village above the Tinée valley. It was missing several parts, notably the eyes, which had probably been enamelled. The animal is stopped in its tracks, standing its ground with its mussel (*hure*) lifted. For the Lug Celts, the boar was the supreme god in their mythology.

*One of three examples of bronze Gallic boars found in France*

Only two other boars from this period have been found in France, one in Loiret and the other in Gironde. At Ilonse, you can now see a cast of the original (which is in the Cimiez archaeological museum at Nice) as well as a reconstruction of the statue.

## SIGHTS NEARBY

### L'ENSEIGNE DU COIFFEUR

Place de l'Église
06420 Saint-Sauveur-sur-Tinée

On the door lintels in place de l'Église, Saint-Sauveur-sur-Tinée, motifs bear witness to the profession of the owners of these properties, some 500 years ago … Although above one of the doors a sheep can be seen, suggesting that a butcher lived in that house, the most unexpected motif is surely the one representing the most indispensable of barber's tools: a comb and a pair of scissors.

## LE SCÉNOPARC ALPHA DE SAINT-MARTIN-VÉSUBIE ㉔

Le Boréon 06450 Saint-Martin-Vésubie
• Tel: 04 93 02 33 69 • www.alpha-loup.com
• Open daily mid-April to end October (hours vary according to season)
• Admission adults €9, children €7

### Are you there, wolf?

The remarkable Alpha* Park in the hamlet of Boréon, 10 minutes from Saint-Martin-Vésubie, is not exactly a zoo in the true sense of the word: the wolves decide if they care to come and see the public rather than the other way round …

Living in enclosures from 2 to 5 hectares in size, depending on species, the wolves are in fact kept in semi-captivity here. Despite these conditions, all you have to do is find out the animals' feeding times and there is a very good chance of observing one or several wolves just a few metres away.

The natural environment is exceptional and the park has been very carefully conceived to maximize the animals' quality of life. Visits are unrestricted and people can move around and observe at their own speed. The three hides with their glazed viewing panels let you get near to the wolves without disturbing them.

Three *scéno-visions* of extraordinary quality (on the themes of pastoralism, science, and of course, the imaginary dimension) explain the hows and whys of wolf myths and realities.

It even seems that the content of these teaching games have created a consensus among sheep farmers as well as "friends" of the wolf. This is important because the natural reappearance of the Italian wolf, in November 1992 in the Mollière valley (kept quiet until mid-1993), provoked reactions right up to

the highest level. The eradication of the wolf in the 1930s and 1940s had indeed made people forget the danger that the animals represented and their reappearance in a world where sheep had replaced cattle was not taken lightly by all stockowners.

During the winter of 2005–06, five wolf cubs were born in the park.

(*) The name Alpha (first letter of the Greek alphabet) was chosen for the park because to scientists this term designates the dominant animal of the pack.

## MADONNA OF NOTRE-DAME-DE-FENESTRE

06450 Saint-Martin-Vésubie • Distance 12 km, access via RD94
• Église Saint-Martin • Rue de l'Église 06450 Saint-Martin-Vésubie
• Chapelle des Pénitents-Blancs • Rue du Docteur-Cagnoli dite rue Ducale
06450 Saint-Martin-Vésubie• Opening hours can be checked at the tourist
office of Saint-Martin-Vésubie, place Félix-Faure • Tel: 04 93 03 21 28

> *The statue, sculpted by Saint Luke, is said to have been brought back by Mary Magdalene*

Following a concurrence of unusual and miraculous facts, pilgrimages to Notre-Dame-de-Fenestre are among the most important in the Alps.

A phase of rivalry between France and Italy was the origin of the name Fenestre [window]. Some Italians, seeking to possess the chapel's Madonna statue, stole it and took it to their own church. But the Madonna, not going along with that, regained her sanctuary of her own accord, taking a shortcut over the mountains and leaving an opening in the rock in the form of a window or "Heaven's door".

Another hypothesis recalls the Latin term *fines terrae* (land's end), evoking the border between the countries.

The statue itself, carved in Lebanese cedar, is said to have been made by Saint Luke, then brought to Provence by Mary Magdalene.

The chapel, constructed by the Benedictines, passed into the hands of the Templars who succeeded them in 1136. Although it suffered four catastrophic fires, each time the statue emerged unscathed. In 1789, for example, when the revolutionaries burned the ex-votos, the statue, hidden at someone's home, escaped the flames.

A number of miracles have been claimed, the most celebrated being the healing of Marie-Jeanne-Baptiste de Savoie-Nemours on15 August 1668. Each summer, the sculpture is taken to Notre-Dame-de-Fenestre chapel where French and Italians still meet up during pilgrimages. In winter it is in theory returned to the church of Saint-Martin, but at present and until an as yet unspecified date, the Madonna can be seen in the chapel of the Pénitents-Blancs (see page 87), just behind the tourist office in rue Ducale.

**SIGHTS NEARBY**

Rue du Docteur-Cagnoli dite rue Ducale

The barber's house, dating from the Middle Ages, is an example of a building serving both as accommodation and site of professional activity. A barber formerly occupied the premises, hence the name.

# LA CHAPELLE SAINTE-CLAIRE

Place Saint-Jean
06450 Venanson

**27**

> ## The life of Saint Sebastian in comic strip

I n the middle of the village of Venanson, from which there is a magnificent view of the valley, it is hard to miss the little Sainte-Claire chapel (also known as the Saint-Jean or Saint-Sébastien chapel). To visit just ask for the key at the grocers or the Bella Vista restaurant in the same square.

Although the exterior of the chapel is nothing special, the interior is superb, decorated throughout with frescoes by Jean Baleison. Painted in the 15th century, they splendidly evoke the life and death of Saint Sebastian. The very graphic details are surprising enough: the saint's body being thrown into a sewer by his executioners and his remains brought out at the request of Saint Lucine in order to give him a more worthy burial place.

The most interesting frieze has unfortunately been largely destroyed. The procession of vices can be seen, but only sloth remains, represented by a prince mounted on an ass.

The chapel of Venanson is one of the numerous chapels of the Alpes-Maritimes hinterland, all equally original in their decoration and the treatment of religious themes. This was a case of teaching religion and morality to a population most of whom could not read, hence the profusion of frescoes, the comic strips of the time, intended to present religious texts in a simple and graphic manner.

---

### SAINT SEBASTIAN

Born at Narbonne in AD 250, Sebastian gained the confidence of the emperor Diocletian, but was denounced as a Christian and pierced by a number of arrows (a scene liberally represented down through the centuries). Sebastian then miraculously presented himself before the emperor, arrows in hand, and dared to criticize his treatment of Christians, which led to a second torture by beating, which this time killed him.

# L'ÉGLISE SAINT-MICHEL-DU-GAST

Place des Anciens-Combattants
Quartier La Bourgade
06450 Roquebillière
• Mado Nésic Perichon organizes captivating guided tours, highly
recommended (Tel: 04 93 03 45 62)

> **An esoteric
> church?**

Saint-Michel-du-Gast church has an impressive collection of esoteric, Masonic,
Templar and Hospitaller symbols. Transferred
to the Hospitallers of St John of Jerusalem in
1141, it was reconstructed in 1533. On the wall
below and to the right of the clocktower, a 666 is preceded by a recent "1", probably added by a 4×4 rally competitor ... The columns, of Roman origin, have
been reused and the entrance door is surmounted by a Templars' cross. The
splendid baptistery in Queyras volcanic rock is decorated with a six-branched
cross symbolizing man, angels, seraphim (see page 69), and the animal, vege-
table and mineral worlds, with God at the centre.

The fourth aisle on the left has a surprising painting of the Apocalypse with
a great number of Masonic symbols. Each detail has been placed with precise significance and the work has acquired a certain renown among the bro-
thers. On the wall of the last aisle to the left, a painting shows Saint Helen, mother of the emperor Constantine, and to the side, Mary Magdalene with a child
... Another unusual element is the sun carved on one of the column capitals,
which receives the rays of the sun at the spring equinox.

Finally, the highlight of the visit is the opening of a long chest at the back
of the church, in which appears a bleeding Christ, terrifying in its realism. It is
said to have been "moulded" on the body of a real person. Mado claims that she
has seen miracles happen in the presence of this hyper-realistic portrayal.

## KNIGHTS OF MALTA

The Sovereign Military Hospitaller Order of St John of Jerusalem, of
Rhodes and of Malta, also called the Knights of Malta, was the second
military order of the Holy Land after the Templars. The founding act of
the order was a hospital for pilgrims, set up towards 1080 at Jerusalem.
Today it is a Roman Catholic organization with sovereign status and
a humanitarian vocation, headquartered in Rome on Via dei Condotti.
These premises and the Aventin Palace enjoy extraterritorial status
that allows the order to maintain diplomatic relations with 94 nations.
It is also recognized by the United Nations, where it has a permanent
observer. For further details, see the title *Secret Rome* published in this
series of guides.

# CANNES, ANTIBES, SAINT-PAUL-DE-VENCE AND SURROUNDINGS

# THE BRIGANDS' TOWER OF LES DANYS

10, rue de Cannes 06110 Le Cannet
• Access: the tower is on private land, but the owner allows free access outside.

When Prosper Mérimée, on a trip to inspect the national heritage,* asked an old woman the name of the tower standing before him, she, speaking only Provençal, replied: *"Ah Moussu! Es habitado per aqueu brigand d'Agnelin s'enebrio chasque jou."* [Ah Monsieur! It's the home of that bandit Agnelin who gets drunk every day.]

> *When Prosper Mérimée failed to understand Provençal ...*

Mérimée, having understood just about one word, *brigand*, baptized the tower "Tour des Brigands".

This name was perfectly suited to the building, where the entrance was situated 3 m above the ground and there were no stairs between the three levels: apparently you had to reach the various floors by ladder. A door at ground level has recently been added.

We know now that this tower, dating from the mid-15th century, was built by the monks of Lérins. It served to block the access to the city and its defensive nature is borne out by the crenellations and lack of openings. In fact it is named after the former district: the hamlet of Danys. The square tower is 9 m high and 5.35 m wide. The base of the walls is around 70 cm thick.

* The French dramatist, historian, archaeologist, and master of the short story served in the mid-19th century as general inspector of historical monuments.

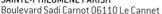
## SIGHTS NEARBY

### SAINTE-PHILOMÈNE PARISH
Boulevard Sadi Carnot 06110 Le Cannet

The parish of St Philomène is, strangely enough, dedicated to a saint who no longer features in the calendar of saints' days. Canonized by a decree of Pope Gregory XVI on 13 January 1837, her feast day fell on 11 August. But in 1961, Philomène was struck from the list of forenames for baptism by the Roman Catholic Church's Congregation of Rites, which considered that the legend based on the life of the young Roman girl was false. This dated from the 19th century: in May 1802 in Rome, during an archaeological dig in the catacomb of St Priscilla, three funerary tiles were found on which could be read: *Pax tecum, Philumena* [Peace unto you, beloved]. The skeleton laid to rest there was that of a young girl of about 15, beside her a broken flask that had contained blood, a common early Christian rite. A priest from Mugnano, near Naples, insisted on exposing these relics and they gave rise to a great number of miracles.

It was on the advice of Jean-Marie Vianney, known as the "Curé d'Ars", that abbot Bovis, the village priest, named this new church built to replace St Catherine's, which had become too small.

## CELL OF THE MAN IN THE IRON MASK, FORT ROYAL ❸

Musée de la Mer
Îles de Lérins
• Embarkation: quai Leaubeuf
• Museum hours: January to March and October to December, 10.30–13.15 and 14.15–16.45; closed Monday. From April to mid-June and mid-September to end September, 10.30–13.15 and 14.15–17.45; closed Monday. From mid-June to mid-September, 10.30–17.45; open daily
• Admission: €3 • Reduced rate: €2

> ### The man in the Iron Mask, great-grandfather of Napoleon?

The cell of the Man in the Iron Mask is the major attraction of the Musée de la Mer. This mysterious prisoner, whose mask was in fact made of leather or velvet rather than iron, was locked up from 1687 to 1698 in a cell that can still be seen today. It was Voltaire who popularized this character, putting forward the hypothesis that he was the brother of the Sun King (Louis XIV). Writers' imaginations soon invented other identities: minister of the Duke of Mantua (Italy) punished for diplomatic indiscretions, priest of the king's household imprisoned for having interfered in his love affairs, natural son of Anne of Austria and Mazarin, offspring of Louis XIII's physician who had been hidden away so as not to reveal the king's sterility … And to embroider the legend, a child fathered by the "Iron Mask" during his captivity was said to have been entrusted to a Corsican family who, convinced that he came from a "good part" (Bona Parte), gave him the family name of Buonaparte. So he would have been the great-grandfather of Napoleon …

Few visitors, on the other hand, know of the writings of Andrew Macdonagh, who in 1777 was imprisoned in this cell for twelve years. During the restoration of the paintings on the cell walls, a bundle of notes was found 2.20 m from the ground, signed Macdonagh. Irish by birth, he was promoted to captain in the French army then imprisoned following an extremely complicated inheritance affair of which he seemed in ignorance. Freed during the Revolution, he supported the cause of Irish independence. His writings were mainly pamphlets denouncing those who had dragged him to this dungeon to rot. Facsimiles of these notes are exhibited in a glass case in the corridor next to the cell.

Other prisoners, more or less notorious, turned up at Fort Royal. Thus there is a memorial to six Protestant pastors who died here in 1687. The Count of Monteil was locked up here for thirty-two years and refused to be set free in 1790 – he felt quite at home … And finally, there was the former Marshal Bazaine who, at the age of 60, managed to escape with the help of a knotted rope held by lieutenant-colonel Wilette (condemned to six months imprisonment for his complicity) and was picked up by a waiting canoe.

## CANNONBALL OVEN, POINTE DU DRAGON ④

Pointe du Dragon
Îles de Lérins
• Embarkation: quai Leaubeuf
• Access: disembarking on the island, go straight on, veering to the right until you come to the junction with the wide allée du Dragon. Follow the alley to the right along to the end where the oven is signposted.

> *Red-hot cannonballs*

Four cannonball ovens, of the dozen that still exist in France, are found in the Lérins islands: two on Saint-Honorat and the two others on Sainte-Marguerite. Built on the orders of the young General Bonaparte, who was designated inspector of the coastal batteries having proved himself as a gunner during the siege of Toulon in late 1793, they completed the defences of the zone.

The oven of the pointe du Dragon is in sufficiently good order to let you understand how it works. The cold cannonballs ran along grooves and piled up in the sloping flue, while from the oven below, where a blazing fire had been stoked up, flames roared through the flue towards the chimney. After an hour of such heating, a red-hot cannonball was ready every 10 minutes, which could instantly set alight the sails or the wood of any ship it was aimed at.

The gunners used special tools such as cannonball pincers to load the guns. Instructions were: "place the charge of powder and tamp it down, add a bung of damp hay or clay, aim, put in the red-hot ball with pincers and light the powder."

The oven is only one of the components of the Dragon battery, which controlled part of the naval approaches to Cannes bay. The emplacement allowed cross-fire with the Braves Gens battery on the island of Saint-Honorat.

### SIGHTS NEARBY

#### THE "UNKNOWN" CANNON ⑤

Discovered in 1995 at a depth of 41 m north of the island of Sainte-Marguerite, a cannon, now displayed at the entrance to the fort, bears the unusual name "Unknown". It is a classic siege cannon, enriched with royal iconography (from the reign of Louis XIV) and the celebrated maxim: *ultima ratio regum* [the last argument of kings].

## THE BENCH IN THE GARDEN OF MUSÉE DE LA CASTRE ⑥

Place de la Castre
06400 Cannes
• Opening hours: October to March 10.00–13.00 and 14.00–17.00; April, May and September 10.00–13.00 and 15.00–18.00; June to August 10.00–13.00 and 15.00–19.00; closed Monday and some public holidays.
• Free access to museum gardens.

> **A marble bench for the haemophiliac son of the British queen**

I n the garden of Castre Museum, a striking text is engraved on a white marble bench: "Peace which the world cannot give. *Érigé par la reine Victoria à la mémoire de son cher fils, le prince Léopold, duc d'Albany, décédé à la villa Nevada le 28 mars 1884. Heureux sont dès à présent les morts qui meurent au Seigneur (apocalypse XIV verse 13)* [Erected by Queen Victoria in memory of her dear son, Prince Leopold, Duke of Albany, died at Villa Nevada on 28 March 1884. Blessed are the dead who from now on die in the Lord (Revelations 14:13)].

On 7 April 1853 Leopold was born, fourth son and eighth child of the British Queen Victoria. It was quickly noticed that he was a haemophiliac and that his life would be cut short by the disorder. A keen scientist and art lover, he had great difficulty in convincing his mother to let him go up to Oxford. It was there that he eventually met Alice Liddell, daughter of the dean, who would inspire his friend Charles Dodgson, better known by his pseudonym of Lewis Carroll, to write *Alice in Wonderland*.

Epilepsy aggravated Leopold's haemophilia, doing nothing to improve his daily routine that was already difficult enough. After several years he finally obtained a peerage, despite his mother's doubts, and became Duke of Albany. He married Hélène, daughter of the Princess of Waldeck, whom it is said he seduced by singing her an Italian love-song. Of their union Alice was born, her name chosen not because of Carroll's work but in memory of one of his sisters …

In 1884 he was staying at Cannes in the Villa Nevada and watching the carnival from the Cercle nautique, when he missed his footing and slipped on the tiled floor. This seemingly harmless incident, because of his haemophilia, in fact caused a cerebral haemorrhage that killed him in the course of the night. As there was no question of letting it be known that a child of Queen Victoria could be afflicted with a hereditary condition, the *Écho de Cannes* laboriously explained in a high-flown style that the Duke of Albany "having no epidermis, such that his flesh, covered with very fine skin, could be affected by the slightest shock".

---

**HAEMOPHILIA**

Haemophilia is a bleeding disorder caused by a deficiency of a substance necessary for blood clotting. The two most typical clinical symptoms are painful bleeding in the joints and bruising of the muscles.

# CARYATIDS OF RUE D'ANTIBES

101, rue d'Antibes
06400 Cannes

The first bared breasts appeared well before the 1960s on Saint-Tropez beaches: from 1882, women were already flaunting their attributes on Cannes buildings. It was in place Vauban, at the beginning of the new boulevard Carnot and at 101 rue d'Antibes that Cannes residents could for the first time see sculptures (by Pellegrini) showing what everyone was hiding at the time. A huge scandal erupted.

*The first bared breasts on Côte d'Azur*

Yet these caryatids were only reproductions of the sculptures of antiquity, modelled on those on the porch of the Erechtheum, on the Acropolis, Athens (see theme of caryatids and atlantes, page 149).

---

### NATURISM AND NUDITY: CÔTE D'AZUR IN THE FOREFRONT

Although the first French naturist club (Sparta Club) was opened by Kienné de Mongeot in 1926, it was doctors André and Gaston Durville who launched the practice in 1930 when they opened Héliopolis, on Île du Levant (in the Hyères group), the first village where you could practise nudism.

Note the important difference in that naturists like to share with others a lifestyle and a state of mind, whereas nudists live alone or in closed circles that are more comfortable for them.

The 1964 film *Le Gendarme de Saint-Tropez* popularized the fashion of the monokini with bared breasts, while stigmatizing the ridiculous side of people's repressive attitudes.

Today there are in France 225 clubs and associations with a total of 85,000 members. If you want to stay at a naturist club or holiday resort, you'll need to join the Fédération Française de Naturisme.

Contact: FFN 5, rue Regnault 93500 PANTIN. Tel: 01 48 10 31 00.

However be warned: Article 222-32/Section III of the penal code equates nudism with exhibitionism and thus is an offence to public decency. Today the law is rarely applied, but certain communes have by-laws banning the practice (you risk a fine).

## TOMB OF JEAN MARAIS
### IN THE VIEUX CIMETIÈRE DE VALLAURIS

Allée du Souvenir-Français 06220 Vallauris
• Opening times: 7.30 from 1 March to 31 October; 8.00 from 1 November to 28 February • Closing times: 17.30 from 1 September to 30 April; 18.00 from 1 May to 31 August
• The tomb is signposted at the entrance to the cemetery. It is located 150 m from the alley leading from the entrance.

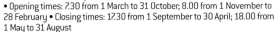

*"Beauty and the Beast"*

Illustrating the theme of Cocteau's *La Belle et la Bête* [Beauty and the Beast], in which Jean Marais plays the beast, his tomb is an astonishing creation designed by the actor himself. Framed by two masks in the image of the beast, it is surmounted by a sphinx with deer's horns and a mermaid's tail. While pursuing his actor's career, Jean Marais had settled at Vallauris and he opened a gallery there in 1975. He died on 8 November 1998.

### SIGHTS NEARBY

#### ESPACE JEAN-MARAIS
3, avenue des Martyrs-de-la-Résistance 06220 Vallauris
• Open 9.00–12.30 and 14.00–17.30. Closed Sunday and Monday. July and August, open daily 10.00–12.30 and 14.00–18.30
• Admission: €1.50

Permanent exhibition of ceramics, sculptures, paintings, photographs, videos.

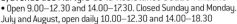

### THE INVENTOR OF THE CÔTE D'AZUR CAME FROM THE CÔTE D'OR

In an impasse (generously called an avenue) between the médiathèque and the railway line, you can admire from the outside the family villa where the "inventor" of the Côte d'Azur spent part of his life. A plaque visible from the street was placed there in 1988 to mark the centenary of the name being coined.

Born on 29 March 1830 at Dijon, Stephen Liégeard had his career mapped out for him as his father was the town's mayor. He did his duty and was nominated subprefect at Briey (Meurthe-et-Moselle), then at Carpentras (Vaucluse), where his neighbour was the writer Alphonse Daudet, who gave him the leading role in his novel *Lettres de mon moulin: Le sous-préfet aux champs* [Letters from My Windmill: The subprefect in the fields]. In 1887, in the middle of winter, he and a friend decided to head for the south coast. Arriving in Hyères before that sea and sky so blue, so pure, so beautiful, he exclaimed "Côte d'Azur!" [azure coast], in reference to the region he came from, the Côte d'Or [golden ridge]. As soon as he returned to Paris, he wrote his major book, *Côte d'Azur*. Published in 1888, the work won the Bordin literary prize awarded by the Académie Française. Liégeard was hooked ... spending more and more time at Cannes, he joined in local life and supported the town, relaunching its scientific and literary society. He died in Les Violettes villa on 29 December 1925. On his memorial they could have added his motto: *Il est beau d'être grand, être bon est meilleur* [It's fine to be great, to be good is better].
Plaque, villa Les Violettes - Avenue Stephen-Liégeard - 06400 Cannes

# EÏCHI AWOKI WORKSHOP

10

15, rue de la Pompe
06600 Antibes

*Do Staël
was here*

I t was in admiration, not to say veneration, of Nicolas de Staël that the Japanese artist Eïchi Awoki left his country and came to France to work near the master, in the Commune Libre [free commune] of Safranier (see inset). In his window, a number of flyers and press cuttings sum up his approach. Just ring and he'll open the door of his workshop, which although tiny is impressive in its ingenuity: for example a very steep stairway made from asymmetrical half-steps leads to the floor above.

Eïchi's painting is greatly inspired by the work of Nicolas de Staël and it seems likely that he has set himself up a few metres from the master's last workshop to capture his vibes. What's more, Eïchi's first walk each morning takes him past the Ardouin mansion, where a plaque recalls that Nicolas de Staël lived there.

## NICOLAS DE STAËL (1914-1955)

In 1954, this French painter of Russian origin (born in 1914 at St Petersburg) settled in Antibes in the Ardouin mansion, located on the ramparts by the sea, promenade Amiral-de-Grasse. Orphaned at a very young age and exiled, he buried himself in painting. Although he studied under Fernand Léger, it was Braque who influenced him more deeply. Having passed the early years of the war in the Foreign Legion, de Staël lived in Paris and then at Ménerbes in the Lubéron. During his time in Antibes, he painted over 300 canvases of landscapes, seascapes, nudes and still lifes, the best-known of which is *Le grand concert*. Nicolas de Staël brought his life to a brutal end on 14 March 1955 when he threw himself from the second-floor window of his workshop.

## LA COMMUNE LIBRE DU SAFRANIER

The aim of this association, set up in the same spirit as the Commune Libre de Montmartre or the Commune Libre des Templiers at Saint-Raphaël (see page 155), is the upkeep of local traditions and the maintenance of links between local residents. The origin of the name Safranier is obscure. It may have come from the *safre* (a friable stone found in the region) quarry which used to be here, or it may refer to *safran*, a boat's rudder blade. The area is today dotted with the association's orange and yellow insignia.

# KAZANTZAKI'S BENCH

Place du Safranier 06600 Antibes

> *"I fear nothing, I hope for nothing, I am free"*

Settling in Antibes in 1948, Nikos Kazantzaki wrote two of his masterpieces there: *La liberté ou la mort* [Freedom or Death] and *La dernière tentation du Christ* [The Last Temptation of Christ]. He liked to come and meditate, finding inspiration on the bench in place du Safranier. Just behind, on a plaque fixed to the wall, you can read the epitaph on his tomb in Crete: *Je ne crains rien, je n'espère rien, je suis libre* [I fear nothing, I hope for nothing, I am free].

## NIKOS KAZANTZAKI

Born at Heraklion on Crete in 1883, Nikos Kazantzaki lived through the revolt of the Cretan people against the Turkish occupation. He studied law in Athens and philosophy in Paris under the guidance of Bergson. After writing a thesis on Nietzsche, he launched a mining venture in the southern Peloponnese with a certain Georges Zorba, an experience that would give rise to his most famous book *Alexis Zorba*, published in 1943 and made into a film in 1964 as *Zorba the Greek*. By the way, the *sirtaki* (composed by Mikis Theodorakis) isn't a traditional Greek dance: created for the film, it played a large part in its success.

# SANCTUARY OF GAROUPE

⑫

Colline de la Garoupe Cap-d'Antibes 06600 Antibes
• Open 10.00–12.00 and 14.30–19.00 (17.00 in winter)
• The ex-votos can be seen on the sanctuary's website: http://garoupe.free.fr

*A pilgrimage, two oratories and over 250 ex-votos*

At the summit of the millionaire's paradise that is Cap-d'Antibes, the humble yet magnificent Chapelle de la Garoupe offers visitors a unique opportunity for contemplation, meditation and unexpected discoveries.

Having admired the sublime panoramic 360° view, you'll find to the left of the chapel the oratory of Sainte-Hélène, dedicated to the mother of the Emperor Constantine. For security reasons, her statue is for the time being inside the sanctuary.

A short distance away is another oratory, that of Notre-Dame-des-Amoureux, created by the illustrator Raymond Peynet who spent many years at Antibes; indeed a museum is devoted to him there.

The most unusual aspect of all this is, however, the exceptional collection of ex-votos in the chapel: pictures dating mainly from the 19th century, tapestries, photographs, drawings, model boats, embroidery, every piece carrying a strong emotional charge. Particularly noteworthy is a black and white photo showing the procession of the patron saint of mariners, on whose hand is written: *En souvenir de mon oncle, premier porteur à droite de la Vierge de Bon-Port* [In memory of my uncle, the first bearer on the right of the Virgin of Bon-Port]. (Every year, on the first Thursday in July, ten seamen with bare feet carry the statue to Antibes Cathedral and bring her back to the sanctuary the following Sunday.)

But the most astonishing ex-voto is perhaps the one that was brought in procession by the municipal councillors in their evening dress, after the collapse of the ceiling of the audience hall during a ball, on 19 February 1822, "only" injuring nineteen people and killing none. The best known, finally, is that of the convict, dating from 1812, giving thanks to the Virgin for having looked favourably on his escape from the slavery of the galleys …

MUSÉE PEYNET ET DU DESSIN HUMORISTIQUE
Place nationale 06600 Antibes • Tel: 04 92 90 54 30
• E-mail: musee.peynet@antibes-juanlespins.com
• Admission € 3. Reduced tarif € 1.50. Free for under 18s.
• Open all year except on Monday and public holidays (1 January, 1 May, 1 November, 25 December), 10.00–12.00 and 14.00–18.00
• Evening sessions in July and August, Wednesday and Friday until 20.00

# LE MONUMENT AU POILU

Fort-Carré
Avenue du 11-Novembre
06600 Antibes
• Tel: 06 14 89 17 45
• www.antibes-juanlespins.com
• Admission € 3, reduced tarif € 1.50. Free for under 18s.
• Open all year except on Sunday, Monday and public holidays
• 16 September to 4 June 10.00–16.30; 15 June to 15 September 10.00–18.00

> **The tallest war memorial in France**

Inaugurated on 8 July 1927, the war memorial of the town of Antibes, 22 metres high, is the tallest in France. Its impressive size thus offers a well-deserved homage to one of the French municipalities to have lost the greatest number of men during the First World War.

It took four years to build this representation of a *poilu* [hairy, unshaven one], as the ordinary soldiers were known, designed by the Antibes architect Edmond-François Copello and sculpted by Henri Bouchard (1875–1960). Critics were up in arms about the location, and the governor Charles de Chavannes, companion of Pierre Savorgnan de Brazza, even wrote a pamphlet condemning the project. But when it was noticed that the soldier held his rifle by his left foot, the anger of war veterans knew no bounds. The rumour was put about that Bouchard committed suicide when he discovered his gaffe, but that proved totally false.

**ANOTHER HOMAGE FROM THE TOWN OF ANTIBES TO THE VICTIMS OF THE FIRST WORLD WAR**

Long before the monument was erected, the municipality had already paid homage to victims of the trenches. You can see in the lobby of Antibes town hall (cours Massena) two wooden dressers with an exhibition of photographs and the names of those who died in action.

**SIGHTS NEARBY**

On the right-hand wall of the *mairie*, near a window, a strange stone is fixed to the wall. On it you can read *Pueri septentrionis Anno XII qui Antipolis in theatro biduo saltavit et placuit*, which may be translated as: "To the child of the north, 12 years of age, who danced two days in the theatre of Antibes with success".

# THE PROPERTY OF MONSIEUR AND MADAME FARINELLI  **15**

Villa Le Pin, 593, chemin du Plan 06410 Biot
• Tel: 04 93 65 05 33 • Visits free, by appointment
• This work is located in a private property and can only be seen by arrangement with the owner. You can ask the Biot tourist office to do this for you. Avoid the siesta hour. Respect the place, don't bring animals along and above all take your children by the hand.
• Access: from the village, take the direction of Antibes, turn left just before crossing the River Brague. Follow the river and take the Plan road until it turns back towards the village.

*Italo
in Wonderland*

**F**ormer mason and stonecutter Italo Farinelli retired some twenty years ago. Wanting to tidy up the stones in his various building sites and lying around his garden, Italo had the superb idea of using them decoratively. Little by little, with an enthusiasm and infinite patience that belied his advancing years, he has built a veritable miniature village.

The group of buildings is in itself original, but the "residents" of this village are even more unique. Garden gnomes rub shoulders with Murano glass, a lifelike tiger's head sits next to characters from films, monsters, santons, soldiers, birds, unidentifed objects … a real fairytale.

## SIGHTS NEARBY

### MAUSOLEUM OF THE GOLDEN GOAT  **16**

Chemin de la Chèvre-d'Or 06410 Biot • Access: from the village, take the direction of Antibes, and turn right just after crossing the River Brague, onto the road for Vallauris. After two hairpin bends on a hill, take the right fork. The mausoleum is on the right side of the road. A notice indicates that parking is banned around it.

A highly unlikely monument to find in such a place, the mausoleum of the Golden Goat dominates the pines from its 9 m height. Dating from the 2nd or 3rd centuries AD, this monumental Roman tomb is surrounded by other *tegulae* (tile-roofed) tombs. Unfortunately no further information is available about the person honoured here, nor about those who are buried nearby. The "Golden Goat" was so named in reference to a legend that grew up around this very spot. It is said that in the evenings, in front of a crevice in the rock known by the herdsmen, a goat with golden horns attracted passers-by with its capricious leaps. Drawn into the cave with its tunnels and galleries, such a man would lose his bearings and find himself alone, abandoned by the animal. He would indeed find a treasure of golden ingots, pearls and gold coins, but would die of hunger and thirst, lost in the innermost depths of the labyrinth. The source of this legend is a true story. In 714, a Saracen known the "King of Majorca" buried in this same cave his treasure pillaged in Provence. Obliged to flee the region, he abandoned his precious booty but left a plan of where to find it engraved on a silver (some say golden) bell.

## A PLAQUE FOR A CATASTROPHE

Place de la Catastrophe 06410 Biot

***The unexplained catastrophe***

When you stroll around the streets of the splendid village of Biot, the huge gap between the houses in rue de la Vieille-Boucherie looks a bit surprising. In fact it's an anomaly, the result of the catastrophe the place is named after. A street plaque recounts the tragedy: on 12 June 1898, during the Fête-Dieu, first communions were being celebrated and as was the custom the parents of the communicants invited family and friends to dinner. So that evening, the house of the Pellegrin family was packed.

Around nine in the evening an extraordinary din startled everybody as a cloud of dust spread around the village. For no apparent reason, the façade of the Pellegrin house had just collapsed, dragging down with it the five floors of that building as well as two adjacent houses. All the villagers rushed to help the unfortunate victims buried under the rubble but, despite the arrival of the army, called by telegraph, twenty-three people were killed.

### SIGHTS NEARBY

MUSÉE ASSOCIATIF D'HISTOIRE ET DE CÉRAMIQUES BIOTOISES
9, rue Saint-Sébastien 06410 Biot
- Tel: 04 93 65 54 54
- Open daily except Monday, Tuesday and public holidays, 10.00–18.00 in summer and 14.00–18.00 in winter
- Admission: €2

### BIOT STONE

The abundant presence around Biot of cinerite, a heat-resistant stone of volcanic origin, led to the development of a kiln manufacturing industry, which obviously required such materials. One thing led to another and the town acquired a worldwide reputation in the field of pottery and stoneware. The Biot kilns were exported all around the Mediterranean with their assembly instructions, rather like the modern "kit" (it wasn't feasible to transport the kilns ready assembled because of their volume and weight).

To see and feel cinerite, you only need to walk out into the countryside nearby, the chemin de Roquefort for example. You can reach that by the Valbonne road: just at the exit to the village, turn right at the corner of Notre-Dame chapel. Go straight along chemin de Saint-Julien to its junction with chemin de Roquefort, which you take to the right. The Aspres plateau, where you'll come out, is largely composed of cinerite rock.

# ARTOTHÈQUE ASSOCIATIVE L'ART TISSE    ⑲

14, rue de la Fontaine 06560 Valbonne
- Tel: 04 93 42 04 56 / 06 82 09 88 21
- www.art-tisse.com
- E-mail: art-tisse@wanadoo.fr

*Works
of art on loan*

To impress your friends and make them think your art collection is inexhaustible, there's nothing like a quick visit to the art library of L'Art Tisse. Understanding that you can be an art lover without necessarily having the money, the association has brought together some fifty creative artists whose work can now be loaned.

This costs a reasonable €8, €16 or €24 per month, depending on the size of the work. To borrow, you have to join and buy a card of twelve units at €96 (€120 for twelve units for companies, but delivery is included).

Each month you can therefore return your picture(s) and choose a new one to take away. Ideal for those who tire of something very quickly. The choice of works can be made on site or via the internet, where the association's website gives a biography of each artist.

At the same time, it plays an active part in the artistic life of Valbonne, organizing exhibitions and activities for students, receiving funding to that effect from the commune and the region.

For those who like the idea, there are two similar associations in the Paris region (see the guide *Banlieue de Paris insolite et secrète in this series*).

# THE MINING SCHOOL SUNDIAL

**20**

École nationale supérieure des Mines de Paris
Avenue Albert-Einstein
Les Lucioles
Sophia-Antipolis 06560 Valbonne
• Access: the sundial is just in front of the school entrance.

*A spectacular sundial*

In 1980, the École Nationale Supérieure des Mines de Paris [which trains engineers] launched a competition to design a sundial for the entrance to its Sophia-Antipolis site. Jean Salins, a Marseille professor, beat 170 competitors. He described his project thus: "An open-air dial in concrete and steel, it consists of a concave wall whose generating lines are parallel to the polar axis. Through slits in this structure can be read, at precise hours, the local solar time by the lines visible on the ground."

The most spectacular aspect of the sundial can't unfortunately be seen very often. By means of letters stencilled into the steel, the sun indicates the summer solstice and the winter equinox by projecting onto the ground, for around quarter of an hour when at its zenith, the words SOLSTICE or ÉQUINOXE spelled out in capitals.

Although, since the sundial was installed, trees have grown nearby and project their extraneous shadows, and you need to lay down sheets of paper to see the lettering properly because of the moss, students still come from far afield to observe the phenomenon.

There are some spectacular photographs taken during the equinox and the solstice on the following website: http://perso.wanadoo.fr/cadrans.solaires/cadrans/cadran-mines.html.

## SOPHIA-ANTIPOLIS

In 1969, senator Pierre Laffitte and a group of eminent scientists set up an association to promote an "international city of learning, science and technology" on a 2,400 hectare wooded plateau between Nice, Antibes and Grasse. Sophia-Antipolis was born. The name Sophia was that of the initiator of the project and Antipolis was the name of Antibes in antiquity. Today, over 1,200 businesses and 25,000 employees are based in this technopole. Research centres, universities, high schools, and prestigious names have given the Côte d'Azur another image, based on high technology.

# A DETACHED HOUSE
## AMONG THE TOWER BLOCKS

Marina Baie des Anges
1001, avenue de la Batterie
06270 Villeneuve-Loubet

*The invincible Gaul*

Anyone who knows the residential complex of Marina Baie des Anges must have asked themselves the same question: "How can that detached house have stayed there, completely surrounded and hemmed in by the four gigantic swaying pyramids of the Marina?" The answer is simple: the owners have always refused to sell their plot to the promoters of the famous scheme.

In 1960, Lucien Nouvel, a wealthy pharmaceutical entrepreneur, decided to invest in leisure property and bought 16 hectares of land at Villeneuve-Loubet, between the coast and the railway line. Unluckily for him, one the landowners, Louis Giraud, refused to sell his house, an former arms depot dating from the early 17th century and still marked as a "magazine" (munitions store) on the Cassini map published in 1815.

There began a drawn-out tussle between the promoters and the invincible house-owner. All manner of pressure was brought to bear on him, alternating with tempting financial offers, but nothing was to be done. One day they came close to a major incident when, exasperated, Giraud took out his rifle.

When work began on the first building (the Amiral), the two companies involved got into a dispute and each refused to let the other's vehicles pass. One of them thus had to negotiate a route through with Louis Giraud, who agreed but demanded compensation. Note that the myth of the tollbooth set up where the lorries had to pass through was just that, a myth, and that the compensation was in fact paid in kind: landfill, concrete and building materials.

In 1970 the Amiral building was delivered and in 1993 the entire scheme was completed with the final building, the Baronnet. The two other buildings, the Commodore and the Ducal, finished before the Baronnet, disrupted the original scheme: the initials ABCD were meant to indicate the buildings in order.

Today nothing has changed and the descendants of Louis Giraud have

inherited the right of passage leading to their "Navy magazine" and their little annex, maliciously called "Marinette". All around, 1,300 homes that in the end have attracted permanent residents, most of them retired people, rather than the expected sporting types.

## THE CLOCK OF THE MUSÉE D'HISTOIRE ET D'ART

Place de Verdun 06270 Villeneuve-Loubet (village)
- Tel: 04 92 02 60 39
- Open 9.00–12.00 and 14.00–18.00; Saturday 9.30–12.30
- Admission free

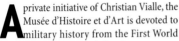

**A clock in a shell**

**A** private initiative of Christian Vialle, the Musée d'Histoire et d'Art is devoted to military history from the First World War to the present. Exhibited on two floors are hundreds of ensigns, military decorations, models, arms, uniforms and artefacts from 20th-century wars. Among the museum's curiosities are an unusual clock, in cast-iron and copper, integrated in a shell that probably dates from 1915. Four twisted bayonets frame this shell. The group recalls the world of Jules Verne and looks ready to take off for the moon …

### SIGHTS NEARBY

### PELOTE PROVENÇALE

The parking opposite the museum (and the annex of the tourist office) is laid out on place De Gaulle. Looking for a space (it's rare to find one), you might be struck by a notice referring to the square as "place du Jeu de Paume". And, if you have good eyesight, you'll see high up on the façade of the building opposite, the front wall of a *pelote Provençale* court dating from 1920. Originally a typical Basque game, it was played in Villeneuve-Loubet, Grasse and Cannes. Developed from the old French game of *jeux de paume, pelote provençale* is known here as *paleta gomme* (played with a ball of dense rubber weighing 480 grams) or *paleta cuir* (with a leather ball). Forty-five permit holders still play *pelote provençale* at Villeneuve-Loubet, on the pelote court of the Jean-Granelle gym at Plans, avenue des Plans.

# PÉTANQUE WITH SQUARE BOULES

Montée de la Bourgade et rue Hyppolite-Guis
World Square Boules Championship 25 August

In the year 1980 Janot Delènne, an active member of the Cercle des Amis and former owner of the Cagnes inn, had an idea: as the streets in uptown Cagnes were too steep and thus not so good for playing *pétanque*, he simply invented a game with square boules!

The rules are appreciably the same as those of the traditional game, except the players use cubes of pine in different colours for each team and the target ball or jack (*cochonnet*), is a plain cube of wood. It is played *pieds tanqués* [your feet don't move] for 13 points to win and the ground is swept in the two streets where the games take place, montée de la Bourgade and rue Hyppolite-Guis. A good game can be had going downhill as well as uphill and a world championship is held each year on 25 August.

In France, Panissières near Roanne, Arvieux in Queyras and Balleray in Morvan, to name but three places, also play this "sport", which requires above all a sense of humour.

> **As the streets were too steep, Cagnes invented pétanque with square boules**

## SIGHTS NEARBY

### 98, MONTÉE DE LA BOURGADE

The house at number 98 montée de la Bourgade conceals an "S" in the wrought-iron work of the staircase. It stands for Simenon (Georges), the creator of commissioner Maigret.

### CHAPELLE NOTRE-DAME-DES-PILOTES

8, chemin Guillaumet

An architect named Balin, who was a keen flyer, decided to build a chapel to perpetuate the memory of the most celebrated airmen from the early days of aviation. On 14 December 1958, Monseigneur Verder, assistant bishop of Nice, laid the first stone of the chapel on land adjoining Monsieur Balin's home. On 29 July 1959, mass was celebrated at the site to commemorate the fiftieth anniversary of the first Channel aeroplane crossing by Louis Blériot but the building work, carried out by the owner and his friends, took a great deal of time – so long that in 1979, after Balin died, the chapel was still unfinished, with structural elements showing.

Today the axis of the chapel nevertheless remains judiciously directed towards Nice airport so the constant air traffic is noticeable. Another result of this initiative is the names of famous airmen given to surrounding streets, such as Guynemer, Nungesser and Coli, Roland Garros, Mermoz or Guillaumet.

# THE FRENCH BRIDGE

**㉗**

Esplanade du Levant (prolongeant la rue de l'Ancien-Pont)
06700 Saint-Laurent-du-Var

> **The River Var marked the border between France and the County of Nice**

From 1814 to 1860, when the region came under the control of Piedmont-Sardinia, the kingdom of the House of Savoy, the Var River (not counted as one of the five rivers of France as it was outside French territory at the time), marked the border between France and the County of Nice.

A bridge was built to link the two banks of the Var at the level of the commune of Saint-Laurent-du-Var. Naturally it was known as the "French Bridge", as the marker still visible today testifies. Moved a few metres and now at the edge of a fence enclosing a rather anarchic parking space, the marker is exactly at the continuation of rue de l'Ancien-Pont. The old bridge failed to resist floods and was breached several times. It lost three arches in 1848, four spans in 1852 and two others in 1855, leading to its final destruction in 1857.

## THE VAR RIVER

"Var" means "water course" in the Ligurian language. Its source is at Entraunes at an altitude of 1,800 m and it flows into the Mediterranean between Nice and Saint-Laurent-du-Var after a journey of 120 km.

The *département* of which the Var is the eastern border takes its name from the river. Today this river flows mainly through the Alpes-Maritimes *département* and brushes Alpes-de-Haute-Provence at Entrevaux. The water level is usually low, but the river is well-known for flash floods, when the flow can pass in a few hours from 100 m$^3$/s to 1,000 m$^3$/s, or even more.

# THE CANNON OF LACAN

Bastion du Dauphin
Porte Nord
06570 Saint-Paul-de-Vence

> *A round*
> *of cherry stones*

**A**lthough the cannon pointing towards visitors arriving in the village of Saint-Paul-de-Vence is well known, few are familiar with its history and the stories told about it.

An authentic 16th-century cannon brought back by the army of Francis I to Saint-Paul in 1544 after the battle of Ceresole d'Alba (Piedmont), this piece of artillery formed part of the fourteen cannons taken from the enemy during the fighting. The French army as it happens had a small contingent of men from Saint-Paul, including an artillery captain named Lacan who, after the French victory, took the cannon back to the village as war booty. Named for its owner, it was added to the defences of the new ramparts.

At the end of the 16th century, "the cannon affair", symbol of the long rivalry between Vence and Saint-Paul, had many repercussions: in order to "wound and humble the pride of Saint-Paul", the villagers of Vence plotted to steal the Lacan cannon, that proud symbol of the Saint-Paulois. One woman from Saint-Paul who lived in Vence got wind of the plot and warned the authorities of her home village. It was then decided to lay a trap for the Vençois. When, in the middle of the night, the latter approached the entrance to the village to steal the cannon, the Saint-Paulois, who had loaded it with cherry stones, lit the fuse. In a thunderous din, a shower of stones rained down on the poor people of Vence. Stained red, they thought they were wounded and fled in a general panic.

Although still told by the village elders, this story is really only a legend.

# ORION BED & BREAKFAST

Impasse des Peupliers
2436, chemin de Malvan 06570 Saint-Paul-de-Vence
• Tel: 06 75 45 18 64 / 04 93 24 87 51
• E-mail: info@orionbb.com • www.orionbb.com
• Rates: €150—245 per night, depending on cabin and number of persons, including breakfast
• Access: from exit 48 of the A8 motorway, take the Vence direction. After 2.5 km, at the third roundabout, turn right towards Vence. 100 m further on, after the fire station and the perfume manufacturers, turn left onto chemin de Malvan. Impasse des Peupliers is 2.4 k from this road.

### Shack up in a cabin

At the foot of the village of Saint-Paul-de-Vence, accessible to the lively Côte d'Azur but far from its bustling crowds, Diane Van den Berge has dreamed up a resort that is quite unusual and unexpected.

Four cabins have been built in the trees around a splendid bathing pond. Very rustic in appearance, the cabins are however equipped with the latest word in comfort: ultramodern sanitation, Wi-Fi connection, minibar, etc. The King Louie cabin, connected to Mowgli cabin by a wooden footbridge, is ideal for a family with children, offering both peace for the adults and fun for the children.

Finally, a footpath is marked out to Saint-Paul village (climbing on the way there, descending on the way back).

## SIGHTS NEARBY

### A BELL FOR A BASKET OF APPLES

Tour de l'Horloge
Place de l'Église
06570 Saint-Paul-de-Vence

Almost impossible to spot from place de l'Église, a bell on top of the donjon (also known as the clock tower) is enclosed in a cage and bears the inscription *Hora est jam nos somno surgere* [The hour has come for you to wake from sleep].

The legend associated with this bell is really amazing: it had in fact been cast in 1443 for the town of Cagnes (now Cagnes-sur-Mer), not for Saint-Paul. It is said that the citizens of Cagnes, ravaged by food shortages, had no other solution but to propose to the Saint-Paulois to swap their bell for a basket of apples. This exchange might have saved Cagnes but nevertheless remained a humiliation difficult to swallow …

Two ways of seeing the bell: go round the church to the left, into rue des Verdalettes, above the ramparts. Otherwise, leave Saint-Paul and go up onto the Colle-sur-Loup with a good pair of binoculars. The tower itself is out of bounds nowadays.

FANNY

# FANNY FROM CAFÉ DE LA PLACE

Café de la Place
Place De Gaulle
06570 Saint-Paul-de-Vence

L ike place des Lices in Saint-Tropez, place De Gaulle in Saint-Paul-de-Vence, with its game of boules and its Café de la Place, is one of the most prestigious *pétanque* pitches in the world.

> *Fanny of Saint-Paul-de-Vence was sculpted by César*

For those that know a little of the rules of this game invented at La Ciotat (see the guide *Secret Provence* in this series), there are two ways of losing a match: a "normal" way by gaining less points than your opponent, and a particularly shameful way by not winning any points at all. This score from 13 to 0 is called "faire Fanny". Tradition has it that the loser, under the mocking laughter of the winners, goes to "kiss Fanny". The said Fanny usually appears as a puppet, kept at the boules club or, as here, at the café next to the pitch. One of the winning team goes to open the curtains and reveal a pair of female buttocks covered with a short white skirt, on which the losers must place a kiss. The distinction of Fanny from Café de la Place is that she was created by the renowned sculptor César and inaugurated on 2 September 1975 by none other than Lino Ventura, who was, with Yves Montand, one of the regular players.

If you want to have a look at Fanny inside the Café de la Place, it would be appreciated if you buy something to eat or drink. You won't regret it: the terrace is the best observation post in the village and the prices are reasonable, taking account of the first-class site. Expect to pay €8 for a *salade niçoise* and €2.20 for a glass of rosé.

---

Saint-Paul-de-Vence tourist office organizes *pétanque* lessons for beginners instructed by a local master of the sport. Rates: €8 per person. Inscriptions and information:
Office de tourisme de Saint-Paul-de-Vence
2, rue Grande 06570 Saint-Paul-de-Vence
• Tél. : 04 93 32 86 95
• E-mail : tourisme@saint-pauldevence.com • www.saint-pauldevence.com

---

### THE ORIGINS OF "FANNY"

The custom of kissing Fanny comes from Savoie. A waitress named Fanny who worked in a café in the town of Grand-Lamps, Sere, let herself be kissed on the cheek to console the humiliated losers of a 13 to 0 match. The day that the mayor presented himself (against whom she apparently bore a grudge) after he'd just been defeated, she refused him her cheek and offered him her buttocks. The mayor wasn't bothered by this and so the tradition started.

# TWO FORGOTTEN ANTIQUE COLUMNS

Place du Grand-Jardin et place Godeau
06140 Vence

### Two columns in one

Now blended into the Vence countryside, two twin columns from antiquity, hewn from the grey granite of Estérel, are hardly noticeable any more.

One is located in the place du Grand-Jardin, in front of the tourist office, and the other in place Godeau behind the cathedral. Some say that these two columns were intended to embellish a triumphal arch erected at Castellane, on the border between Marseille and Vence territories when the road linking the two towns was being relaid. Others say that they formed part of a temple dedicated to the god Mars, which used to stand on the site of the present cathedral. According to the inscriptions engraved on their plinths, they had been offered by the people of Marseille to Vence at the beginning of the 3rd century AD, during the reign of the Roman emperor Caracalla, to celebrate a long tradition of trade between the two powerful and friendly cities. The monument was commissioned by a certain Lulius Honoratus, procurator for the emperor, former centurion and governor of Alpes-Maritimes.

Later, as was the custom, the columns were reused to support the vaulting of the cathedral choir. In 1765, after the building was enlarged, the columns were abandoned. One of them was then used to help hold up the roof of the former fish merchant's shop. In 1910 that establishment was demolished and in 1966 the column was given over to the ornamental role that it fulfils so very well

in place du Grand-Jardin. As for the second column, it was snapped up to decorate what is now place Godeau.

Strangely enough, the reference to the god Mars evoked by these columns sometimes leads to misunderstanding concerning the name of place Antony-Mars, beside the town's ancient ramparts. Antony Mars was a dandy from Vence, composer of operettas during the *belle époque* (late 19th century), and has no connection with the god of war nor with the short form of Marseille in popular use today.

# DONJON OF MALVANS

Quartier du Malvans 06140 Vence

• Access: Allow about an hour for the round trip and wear walking shoes, as the path is stony and uneven. From the town centre, drive out on the Grasse and Tourettes-sur-Loup road. After 1.5 km, turn right onto chemin des Cambreniers. To the right as you go up, near a gateway, lovers of the unusual will notice a niche with a bear and the sign "Berlin: 1,685 km". The track climbs and you should leave the car before the paved road ends. Carry on right up to the chapel. The donjon is just beside it.

> *The chateau of Queen Joan?*

**D**ating from the 12th century, the donjon of Malvans was probably part of a fortified hamlet abandoned at the end of the Middle Ages, probably after a plague epidemic.

Like so many other ruins in the region, this one bears the name chateau of Queen Joan. A tenacious yet magnificent legend links the queen with this place. Joan, more concerned with gallantry (to put it mildly …) than with looking after her realm, is supposed to have stayed here around the year 1350. On Christmas Eve, she was sulking at not having seen her favourite page Aubépin [Hawthorn] join the company,

when he finally arrived. Mad with jealousy, one of the courtiers already present stabbed his young rival before Her Majesty's eyes. Several years later, when Queen Joan returned to the chateau of Malvans, deserted since the tragedy, she discovered a hawthorn bush on the exact spot where Aubépin had been killed. At the stroke of midnight, the bush blossomed with a thousand red flowers … Since then, legend has it, every Christmas Eve a hawthorn bush flowers in the ruins of the Malvans tower.

---

**QUEEN JOAN**

Daughter of Charles, Duke of Calabria and Marie de Valois, Joan I (1326–1382), known as Queen Joan but also countess of Provence, of Forcalquier and of Piedmont, reigned over Naples, Sicily and Jerusalem. She spoke no Latin, however, which stopped her understanding any of the acts she signed … Of great beauty and remarkable spirit, she had an insatiable sexual appetite, married several times and was finally strangled on the orders of her cousin Charles of Durazzo (Charles III of Naples). She only came once to Provence (visiting Avignon), but each town and village claims to have sheltered her within its walls …

# STATUE OF EUGÈNE SUE

Place Eugène-Sue 06480 La Colle-sur-Loup

> *Eugène Sue*
> *is looking at me ...*
> *Je t'aime*

Sculpted by local artist Théo Giordan for the centenary of writer Eugène Sue's death and inaugurated in 1954, the statue recalls the La Colle origins of his family. It was unveiled by Simone Signoret because of a pleasing anecdote ... She and Yves Montand spent most of their holidays at the legendary hotel La Colombe d'Or at Saint-Paul-de-Vence, just opposite La Colle, which they often passed through on their way to the hotel. In 1950, Yves Montand recorded the famous sketch *Le télégramme*, in which he dictated to the post office clerk the celebrated phrase:

"The statue is still in the same place, Eugène Sue is looking at me ...

– Eugène, like the forename?

– Yes ...

– And then?

– Sue ... Eugène Sue

– Spell it."

A year later, he married Simone Signoret at Saint-Paul.

---

### EUGÈNE SUE (1804-1857)

Son of a family of doctors originating from La Colle-sur-Loup, Eugène Sue became a naval surgeon and left the service six years later. From 1831 he lived in Paris where he frequented Alexandre Dumas, Honoré de Balzac and Stendhal. Heir to a large fortune, he lived on his private income and wrote his first works: plays, sea stories, adventures, comedies of manners and period pieces. It was however his serials such as *Les mystères de Paris* [The Mysteries of Paris] and *Le Juif errant* [The Wandering Jew] that gained him huge popularity. In 1844, he left Paris for Orléans and entered politics. Being on the far left of the political spectrum, he was arrested during Napoleon III's *coup d'état* and went into permanent exile at Annecy (Savoie), where he died in 1857.

A curious detail is that the birthdate of Eugène Sue varies according to his biographer, and no less than six different dates have been put forward: 17 January 1803 according to one of his publishers Maurice Lachâtre, 1 January 1803 for Alexandre Dumas, 1 January 1801 for Eugène de Mirecourt (a prolific author and principal detractor of Alexandre Dumas whom he accused of having had his work written by "ghost writers"), 10 December 1804 for journalist Paul Ginisty and 8 February 1804 for Francis Lacassin (essayist and coiner of the term "9th art" for comic strips). According to Jean-Louis Bory (film critic and writer, who became widely known for his cult radio programme *Le masque et la plume*), Eugène Sue was born V Pluviôse Year XII of the Republican Calendar, that is 26 January 1804.

### SIGHTS NEARBY

### A CELL ON THE STREET
26, rue de la Victoire
06480 La Colle-sur-Loup

In the beautiful village of La Colle-sur-Loup, an ordinary door is marked by a strange little sign: "Former prison". Sliding back the heavy bolt, the door opens on a very narrow corridor, with a sloping roof of planks within which a sojourn must have been particularly trying. Despite the name prison, it seems that this is rather a "drying-out cell", where aggressive individuals that have drunk too much could be isolated. This cell was thus merely an annex to the prison of Saint-Paul-de-Vence, which incuded the "Colles" [hillsides], as La Colle-sur-Loup only became an autonomous commune in 1792.

# ST JOHN'S CHAPEL FRESCOES

Chapelle Saint-Jean
Route de Saint-Jean
06140 Tourrettes-sur-Loup

> ## *Reconversion of Ralph Soupault*

In 1959, Ralph Soupault, an illustrator under house arrest at Tourrettes-sur-Loup, offered his services to paint the walls of St John's chapel. He had been condemned to fifteen years of forced labour for collaboration with the Germans in the Second World War but was released early for health reasons. Before and during the war, he had in fact used his talents to help the most unworthy causes of the time. He was put in charge of the Paris PPF (French Popular Party set up by Jacques Doriot), whose black-clad members practised the Nazi salute. Following his release from prison, Soupault found a new life in illustrations for young people and, under the pseudonym Jean-François Guindeau, drew for the comics *Cœurs Vaillants* and *Fripounet et Marisette*. Hergé himself, not knowing of Soupault's past, recommended him to the editor-in-chief of *Tintin* magazine.

The chapel frescoes show biblical scenes and everyday village life. Their originality, other than the naive style, is that they depict the actual inhabitants of the village. So today, the people of Tourrettes can find the faces of departed friends, parents or grandparents.

On the Noah's Ark fresco there also appears the character of Lanza del Vasto, founder of the Communautés de l'Arche. This disciple of Gandhi lived at Tourrettes, where he set up the first of these communities in 1948 with a few of his followers. Finally, above the door of the chapel, a fresco is a reminder that violets are a village speciality.

---

**LANZA DEL VASTO**

Joseph Lanza del Vasto (born 29 September 1901, San Vito dei Normanni, Italy; died 5 January 1981, Murcia, Spain), real name Giuseppe Giovanni Luigi Enrico Lanza di Trabia, was a philosopher, poet and artist (sculpture and drawing). He is best known for setting up the Communautés de l'Arche, which are run on the model of Indian ashrams with the aims of exercise, prayer and work. In 1936 he went to India to meet Gandhi and, at the source of the Ganges in the Himalayas, received his mission: "go back and found". From Palestine to the Causses du Larzac, from the Algerian war to the atomic bomb, Lanza del Vasto thus involved himself in non-violent struggle interspersed with hunger strikes. His novel/travelogue *Le pèlerinage aux sources* (first published by Denoël, Paris, in 1943) was a bestseller.

# FRÉJUS, SAINT-RAPHAËL AND SURROUNDINGS

## LE PORT ROMAIN DE FRÉJUS

• Guided tour by Philippe Cantarel (Fréjus tourist office) • Friday, 17.00 during tourist season • Admission: €5
• Information & reservations:
Office de tourisme de Fréjus
325, rue Jean-Jaurès 83600 Fréjus
• Tel: 04 94 51 83 83 • E-mail: tourisme@frejus.fr • www.frejus.fr

> **The only Roman port in France that can still be seen today**

For those interested in Roman antiquity, Fréjus is a major stopping place, but most visitors generally limit their sightseeing to the arenas, the theatre and the aqueduct. But Fréjus owed its true importance in Roman times mainly to its port.

At a time when all other ports on the southern coast of Gaul were still in Greek hands, Forum Julii provided an anchorage for the Roman fleet. Covering an area of 17 hectares, it would welcome the 300 galleys seized by Octavian from Mark Anthony, Cleopatra's ally, during the battle of Actium off the shores of Greece in 31 BC.

The visit takes you around the wall of this port which has now been filled in: it starts at porte d'Orée, which was not in fact a gate but probably one of the arches in the port's public baths. As for the butte Saint-Antoine, this is an area in the very heart of Fréjus that remains free of recent construction, believed to have been occupied by the official residence of the Roman maritime prefect. The *cloaca* (sewers) are easily spotted in the middle of the ruins, and end in boulevard Séverin-Decuers. Finally, chemin de la Lanterne d'Auguste leads to a curious monument, once supposed to have been a lighthouse but most likely simply a landmark at the port's entrance whose height allowed pilots to line up their vessels during the final approach.

But the most surprising vestige remains the bollard at the very end of chemin de la Lanterne d'Auguste. Carved out of esterellite (a blue porphyrous rock once quarried in the nearby Estérel area), the bollard's base still bears the marks of rubbing from innumerable ships' ropes and today it discourages illicit parking.

Although it's possible to walk along chemin de la Lanterne d'Auguste on your own, it would be a shame to deprive yourself of the knowledge and humour of Philippe Cantarel, the guide from the town's tourist office.

### SIGHTS NEARBY

#### FUNERARY HEXAHEDRON AT THE EDEN PARK RESIDENCE

Résidence Eden Park, Rue Jean-Carrara 83600 Fréjus

When Eden Park was being built in the 1980s, a Roman tomb was unearthed. Dismantled stone by stone and then reassembled a few metres away so that it could be preserved intact, it can be seen from the residence's park, which is open to the public. It contains a funerary urn in the form of a hexahedron and it is partly clad in white marble.

## A WALK THROUGH THE REMAINS OF THE MALPASSET DAM ❸

Exit 48 from the A8 motorway, direction Féjus-Centre
At the first roundabout (Galagon), turn left in the direction of Malpasset. Drive on for 5 km on and leave your vehicle in the car park just beyond the piers of the motorway bridge. A private venture housed in a shack sells a guide with the history of the dam and offers to accompany visitors. Walk up the path and allow for an hour's journey to the foot of the dam and back again.

O n December 1959, at 9.13 in the evening, a series of low cracking sounds alerted the population around Fréjus that something was amiss. The Malpasset dam had just given way and released 50 million m³ of water in a 40 m high wave that rushed down upon the town at a speed of 70 km per hour. The disaster took 423 lives, and André Coyne, the engineer who had designed the dam, died six months afterwards.

> *In 1959, the Malpasset damspilled 50 million m³ of water on top of Fréjus ...*

But it seems that it was not the design of the dam (an arched dam, a type reputed for solidity, although in this case the arch was slender) which was to blame for the catastrophe, but rather the fragility of the rock on which the construction rested. In this winter of 1959, torrential rains had filled the reservoir too quickly for the water level to be regulated. And construction work on the motorway bridge prevented the water from flooding the Reyran riverbed instead of the town.

Fifty years have gone by, yet even today as you come round a bend you see blocks of concrete weighing several tonnes, remains of the dam, a gaping wound that seems to cling desperately to the injured rock. But nature has for the most part reconquered the Reyran valley, seemingly indifferent to this human tragedy.

Two other itineraries also let you view the ruins of the Malpasset dam, and are described in a leaflet available from Fréjus tourist office.

OFFICE DE TOURISME DE FRÉJUS
325, rue Jean-Jaurès 83600 Fréjus
• Tel: 04 94 51 83 83 • Mail : tourisme@frejus.fr • www.frejus.fr

# MISSIRI MOSQUE

Rue des Combattants-d'Afrique-du-Nord, RD4, 83600 Fréjus
• The mosque itself (surrounded by a barbed-wire fence) is not accessible, but
can be viewed from the exterior.

> *A mosque built by Senegalese infantrymen*

The initiative taken by Indochinese soldiers serving in the French Army in building a pagoda in order to practise their religion (see page 151) was imitated a little later by the Senegalese infantrymen of Muslim faith.

Completed in 1930, it is a copy, slightly reduced in size, of the Missiri mosque in Djenné, a town in the middle valley of the Niger in Mali. The project went ahead thanks to the efforts of Captain Abdel Kader Madenba, who lodged a complaint with his superior, Colonel Lainé: "The Annamites have their temple, the Madagascans their theatre, but we Senegalese have nothing." The atmosphere of the mosque was even enhanced with African huts and fake, but realistic-looking, termite hills.

## SIGHTS NEARBY

### THE ATLANTES OF RUE SIÉYÈS
53, rue Siéyès 83600 Fréjus

Walking along rue Siéyès in Fréjus, it is difficult to miss the extraordinary door framed by two immense atlantes bearing loads in the manner of *portefaix* (as porters used to be called). Contrary to most such figures, these are not holding up a balcony, since this private townhouse, built in the 17th century by the lieutenant-general of the Fréjus admiralty, François Vaixière (who served at this post from 1665 to 1687), has none. The twin atlantes are also unusual in being *engainés*, meaning that their lower limbs are enclosed in sheaths.

Finally, a closer look at this exceptional door frame reveals an even bigger surprise: the face one sees just above the centre of the door is more reminiscent of a faun (a creature embodying the vital force nature, akin to the Greek satyr) than a "normal" human, and ... he's sticking out his tongue!

### ATLANTES AND CARYATIDS

It is customary for the statues of men supporting great weights to be called "atlantes" (the plural of "atlas"), while those of women are termed "caryatids". Atlantes are a reference to Atlas, the Titan who carries the world on his shoulders.

As for caryatids, they derive their name from the Greek word *karuatides*, which refers to the women of Karue (Caryae), a town in the Greek Peloponnese peninsula. During the Persian Wars, it sided with the Persian invaders against Athens and other allied Greek city-states, which in revenge for this treason slaughtered the male inhabitants and enslaved the women, forcing them to bear heavy loads. According to another hypothesis, the women themselves served as models for the first statues of this kind.

# HÔNG HIÊN BUDDHIST PAGODA ❻

13, rue Henri-Giraud 83600 Fréjus
• Tel: 04 94 53 25 29
• E-mail: pagodehonghien@yahoo.com
• Opening hours: 9.00–12.00 and 14.00–18h (17.00 from September to April)
• Admission: € 1.50, free for children under 7

*The biggest reclining Buddha in Europe*

Considering Fréjus' military past, the presence of a Buddhist pagoda in this town is not so surprising. When France had large number of colonial recruits in the ranks of its army, it was not easy to train them to fight in a country so different to their homeland. Fréjus therefore served as a transitional staging-post between the warm, humid climates of most of the colonial territories and the often freezing conditions found on the battlefields in the north. Thus many of the Vietnamese soldiers who came to fight at the side of Frenchmen during the First World War stayed here.

In order to have a place of worship corresponding to their religious beliefs, in 1917 the men of the 4th colonial infantry regiment decided to build the Hông Hiên pagoda. Transformed and enlarged in 1972, the pagoda is located close by the Indochina war memorial, where since 1987 the repatriated bodies of the soldiers and civilians who died in the service of France now lie.

The visit only allows you to stroll in the garden, access to the interior being reserved to practising Buddhists. The most spectacular statue is that of the reclining Buddha (the biggest of its type in Europe), which is 10 m long and made from concrete. Along the garden's alleys, visitors will also encounter various other figures from Buddhist mythology, whose bright colours may be surprising. Finally, the monumental bell towers over passers-by with its height of 2.5 m and weight of 2 tonnes.

# MENHIRS, DOLMENS
### AND THE HEALING STONE AT SAINT-RAPHAËL

*The healing stone*

Saint-Raphaël has a number of prehistoric remains that are not always easy to find in its highly urbanized landscape. Four of them, dating from the Neolithic Period (6000–2300 BC), are worth a visit.

The menhir at Aire-Peyronne is a block of red porphyry 2 m high, engraved with 200 cupules. These holes hollowed out by human hand are among the most ancient signs carved on stone. In the past, this monolith was called the "healing stone" due to the salutary properties attributed to it. Conversely, it is said that a young woman, herself a doctor of medicine, once allowed herself to be photographed sitting on top of the stone, wearing a mocking smile that betrayed her scepticism. The following day she suffered from acute and inexplicable pains on the very spot where her body had come into contact with the stone... The menhir at the Veyssières roundabout, at the start of boulevard Kennedy, has a signpost reading: "Cultural monument made from Permian sandstone, erected in the Chalcolithic Age, 4500 years ago."

After various adventures, including its transfer to Draguignan, the other menhir at Les Veyssières has returned to Saint-Raphaël. It now stands in the courtyard of the Musée d'Archéologie Sous-Marine et de Préhistoire. A human head and a serpent are sculpted on one of its faces.

Lastly, the Valescure dolmen is composed of six large standing stones with no horizontal slab and can be found in the garden of the Hôtel Latitudes. If you ask at reception, the staff will be pleased to show you where it is.

---

In breton dolmen means "stone table" and menhir means "long stone".

---

**Menhir d'Aire-Peyronne**: RD100, 83700 Saint-Raphaël
• Access: from the Aspé roundabout (next to the cemetery of the same name), take the RD100 (a no-through road) in the direction of the Grand Caous quarry. After reaching this quarry, drive on for another 1.5 km. In a small pass, you'll see two tracks to the right and left, both closed by barriers. The menhir is a few metres along the right-hand track.

**Menhir des Veyssières**: Veyssières roundabout 83700 Saint-Raphaël
• Located beside the roundabout.

**Second menhir at Les Veyssières**: Musée d'Archéologie Sous-Marine et de Préhistoire, Place de la Vieille-Église 83700 Saint-Raphaël • Tel: 04 94 19 25 75
• Opening hours: Tuesday to Saturday, 9.00–12.30 and 14.00–17.30. Closed Sundays, Mondays and holidays. July and August, 10.00–12.30 and 14.30–19.00; Thursday closing time 21.00; Sunday 18.00. Closed Mondays and public holidays. Annual closure in November. • Admission free.

**Dolmen de Valescure** : Hôtel Latitudes Boulevard Darby Valescure 83700 Saint-Raphaël • Tel: 04 94 52 68 00

# THE DAISIES

**8**

## OF THE NOTRE-DAME-DE-LA-VICTOIRE-DE-LÉPANTE BASILICA

Place du Parvis-Jean XXIII Boulevard Félix-Martin 83700 Saint-Raphaël
- Guided tour: "La Belle Epoque in Saint-Raphaël", visit beautiful buildings
- Information and reservations at the municipal tourist office
Office municipal de tourisme Quai Albert-Ier BP 210 83702 Saint-Raphaël Cedex
- Tel: 04 94 19 52 52  E-mail: information@saint-raphael.com

*When the architect signed with a daisy ...*

The impressive size of the Notre-Dame-de-la-Victoire-de-Lépante basilica fully captures Saint-Raphaël's spirit at the end of the 19th century. Completed in 1883 in a neo-Byzantine style, the edifice was so named at the request of Pierre Aublé, its architect. The scion of an old family from Lyon, he was nevertheless born on Rhodes, an island that played a role in the famous battle of Lepanto (1571). A coalition of Christian countries, led by Venice, won a great victory there over the Turks of the Ottoman Empire. Pierre Aublé was a member of a generation of French engineers who were charged with supervising large-scale colonial projects in the Middle East. Upon his return to France, he was recruited by Félix Martin, mayor of Saint Raphaël, whose ambition was to turn his town into a new and prestigious seaside resort, leaving Fréjus to its Roman ruins. Pierre Aublé, out of necessity, became an architect and in addition to the basilica, he built more than 150 villas (of which 40 still remain standing). They resemble one another and were built in the so-called "para-Palladian" style, in reference to the work of the Italian Renaissance architect, Palladio. Aublé made great use of colonnades, loggias, stairways, and patterns borrowed from antiquity, decorating his cornices with painted friezes.

Like many architects, Pierre Aublé insisted on putting his signature upon his buildings. He did so in a subtle manner, in each of his constructions there are one or more daisies – *marguerites* in French – an allusion to his wife's first name.

In the basilica, the daisies form a mosaic decorating the floor of the central bay.

### THE BATTLE OF LEPANTO

This battle for hegemony in the Mediterranean opposed a Christian fleet, consisting of ships from Spain, Venice, Genoa, and Pisa, as well as those of the Knights of Malta, to the Ottoman navy.

The battle ended in a complete rout of the Turkish forces, which lost 260 of the 300 vessels in their fleet, along with 30,000 men and 39 standards. For France, an ally of the Ottoman Empire, it also represented a defeat, which explains why there are no streets named after Lepanto in French towns ... except in Nice, an Italian city until it was annexed by France in 1860.

A basilica is a Catholic church that has been honoured by a particular event or circumstance (miracle, place of pilgrimage, etc.) and enjoys special ceremonial rights. Only the Pope may promote a church to the rank of basilica.

# THE FREE COMMUNE OF THE TEMPLARS

Mairie de la Commune Libre des Templiers
54, rue des Templiers
83700 Saint-Raphaël
• Tel: 04 94 82 25 05 / 06 80 73 04 43

*A zany commune*

Since 1998, there has been a free commune in Saint-Raphaël that does not advocate separatism but instead aims to instil a state of mind in the town that strongly tends towards zaniness. Adhering to the same Charte des Communes Libres to which Belleville and Montmartre in Paris both belong, the "CLT", as it is called here, devotes itself to introducing strangers to local rites and incidentally reducing their fellow citizens to helpless laughter.

Among the numerous events organized by the CLT, we mention the *Transat en sanitaire*, a nautical race whose rules stipulate that the vessel must be a bathtub. Another very popular competition is the bed race, where the pilots, who must be lying down, are not allowed to fall asleep. And of course, not forgetting their famous *pétanque* tournaments with square boules (see page 131 Cagnes-sur-Mer), which certainly make a change from the daily rounds!

All these events build a highly convivial atmosphere that invariably concludes with a banquet following these harebrained competitions. But the association offers some genuinely educational activities as it holds lessons each week teaching Provençal or how to play the *galoubet* (the traditional Provençal flute). But we hasten to add that in addition to these serious classes there are some rather dafter subjects such as workshops on constructing unidentified modes of transport (floating bathtubs, bicycles without wheels, ostriches, etc.)

The "Commune" has staked out its territory around rue des Templiers (which owes its name to the fact that it is located opposite the Templiers church, currently being restored) and several street plaques prove that it really exists. One of them even makes gentle fun of the official plaques rendering homage to the heroes of the Résistance.

Detail of façade of association's premises

# ÎLE D'OR

83700 Saint-Raphaël

*Tintin's
Black Island?*

W hen discovering the Île d'Or, only a
stone's throw from the mainland to
the east of Saint-Raphaël, opposite Le Dramont beach, an assiduous reader of
Tintin's adventures will inevitably think of the
cover of Hergé's album *The Black Island*, although if may remind some of Île
Noire, site of the Morlaix lighthouse in Brittany.

Sold at auction by the French state in 1897, Île d'Or was by a certain
Monsieur Sergent for 280 francs. It is said that after a *bouillabaisse* supper with
plenty to drink, he then lost it playing cards. It was the next owner, Dr Auguste
Lutaud, who built the Saracen-style tower, with a square cross-section, as opposed to most of the other towers in the region that conform to the round
Genovese model. In 1912, his work complete, Dr Lutaud declared himself "king
of Île d'Or", under the name of Auguste the First. He minted money and issued
postage stamps. After his death (his ashes remain on the island, in a grave facing out to sea), Monsieur François Bureau, a naval officer, bought the island in
1961. He perished during his daily swim around his property.

The island is still in private hands today and the owners, when they are in
residence, raise a flag to advertise the fact. There is no transport service to the
island and owners ask that anyone who nevertheless lands there to please take
their rubbish with them when they leave..

## SIGHTS NEARBY

### A VOLCANO ON THE BEACH: THE ROCKS OF LES LIONS BATTERY

Chemin du littoral 83700 Saint-Raphaël

• Access by the car park just after the port of Santa-Lucia. The rocks are to be
found at the very beginning of the trail along the coast.

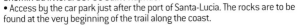

The two tiny islands know as *"Lion de
terre"* [Land lion] and *"Lion de mer"*
[Sea lion], observed at the beginning
of the coastal trail, have some surprising geometric patterns. These prisms,
which look like pipes when seen in pro-
file, and a wall of regular-shaped stones
viewed head-on, are in fact blocks of so-
lidified lava, the volcanic activity in the
region (some 60 million years ago) having released flows of lava from chim-
neys. This type of stone, called  trachy-
te, is a close cousin of rhyolite (see page
158 regarding the millstone quarry at
Bagnols-en-Forêt).

## MILLSTONE-CUTTING WORKSHOPS AT BAGNOLS ⑫

GR51, 83600 Bagnols-en-Forêt

• **The tourist office** at Bagnols-en-Forêt can provide you with a map along with a brochure on the subject of millstones, and techniques for grinding grain and olives. • Access: Allow about two hours for a return journey on foot to see the cutting workshop. We advise sturdy footwear. To reach the site from Bagnols-en-Forêt, take the RD47 towards Notre-Dame chapel. Park in cemetery parking space just beyond the chapel and follow the wide track closed to traffic. 900 m further on, turn right at the fork with a sign pointing to: "Tailleries de meules et col de la Pierre de Coucou". Once you reach the Pierre de Coucou pass, turn right onto the track marked GR51 and walk up it, following the signs indicating *carrière des meules* (millstone quarry). After a fairly long climb, the first millstones start to appear on both sides of the track.

### Grinding it out ...

The site of the millstone-cutting workshop at Bagnols is particularly moving. The stones that were in the process of being extracted have been left in place, still embedded in the rock, as if the quarrymen had suddenly been interrupted in the middle of their work. A branch of the Grande randonnée GR trail to the left leads to a balcony overlooking Fréjus and the rocky knoll of Roquebrune. It is there that you will

find two of the most "beautiful" specimens of millstone: with a diameter of 60 cm, they date from the Gallo-Roman era and were intended for family grain mills. Most of the other millstones that can be seen here, with diameters ranging from 90 cm to 160 cm, were used in oil or wheat mills. You can also find extracted grinding basins, the other half of the millstone, as it were.

The quarry was worked until the Middle Ages, and probably interrupted activity in 1393, the year when the village was abandoned due to epidemics and armed raids. Production later resumed from the 15th to the 18th centuries. But the massive importation of millstones from Spain (these were called *Barcelones*) Holland, and Savoy, brought about the definitive closure of the cutting workshop at Bagnols. Of lower quality, because the rock was softer and hence did not last as long, these imported millstones cost six times less ...

*Rhyolite is a stone of volcanic origin, of which the variety known as amaranth is the major component of the Estérel massif. It is as hard as granite..

---

OFFICE DE TOURISME DE BAGNOLS-EN-FORÊT
Place de la Mairie 83600 Bagnols-en-Forêt
• Tel: 04 94 40 64 68 • E-mail: bagnols-en-foret.tourisme@wanadoo.fr
• www.officedetourismebagnolsenforet.com

### THE FONDURANCE AQUEDUCT
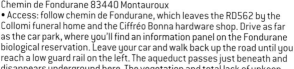

Chemin de Fondurane 83440 Montauroux

• Access: follow chemin de Fondurane, which leaves the RD562 by the Collomi funeral home and the Ciffréo Bonna hardware shop. Drive as far as the car park, where you'll find an information panel on the Fondurane biological reservation. Leave your car and walk back up the road until you reach a low guard rail on the left. The aqueduct passes just beneath and disappears underground here. The vegetation and total lack of upkeep means you'd need a machete to get anywhere near it, but you can see a section about a metre wide, as well as the entrance to the tunnel that eventually flows into Saint-Cassien lake.

The aqueduct of Fondurane was part of the first primitive aqueduct serving Roman Fréjus (Forum Julii), bringing water from the springs at La Foux into town. Later, it proved inadequate to meet the needs of the rapidly expanding settlement and this led to the tapping of water supplies from the source of the Siagnole River near Mons (see page 163) The Siagnole aqueduct joined with the one from La Foux just before this visible section, although the precise location of the junction is still unknown. It may very well be that other secondary aqueducts also fed into the main viaduct.

---

TO FIND OUT MORE

An internet site created by Monsieur Vito Valenti presents a fascinating and very complete study of the Fréjus aqueduct: http://traianus.rediris.es/textos/frejus_fr.htm

---

# THE LITTLE GOOD-LUCK PIG OF CALLIAN &#9899;14

Tour de l'Horloge
Rue du Château
83440 Callian

> *A pig's
> head with
> a snout polished
> by thousands
> of hands*

**C**allian, a magnificent village typical of Var, forms a spiral pattern around a (private) medieval chateau, rebuilt in the 17th century. One of the edifice's two towers boasts a clock [*horloge*] that gives it its name. At the tower's base, a door with a decorated lintel that may pass unnoticed also boasts a pig's head. Over time, its snout has become polished from the caresses of thousands of hands, since, as the small sign next to it tells you, this snout supposedly brings good luck ... :

*Ô toi qui viens de loin,*
*Si tu frottes mon groin,*
*À coup sûr, très grand bien*
*À jamais sera tien.* \*

In 1958, Henri Briffaut, who had been the tutor of Baudouin, King of the Belgians, when the latter was a young prince, found himself enchanted by the ruins of château de Callian. He acquired the property and restored it with respect and good taste, winning several awards. A painter, writer and sculptor, Briffaut placed several examples of his own creations here and there: the imaginary animals standing along the ramparts like somewhat dreamlike contemporary gargoyles, but also, in front of the little door to the chateau on rue de Lyle, a stone knight bearing a cross potent (see box), and of course the realistic pig's head on the door of the clock tower.

---

**THE CROSS POTENT**

Also called a Jerusalem cross, the cross potent represents the instrument of public execution in use during the first years of Christianity. It was adopted as an emblem by the Knights Hospitaller of St John of Jerusalem. French boy scouts wear the cross potent in memory of Jerusalem, the birthplace of the Christian religion.

---

\*Oh you who come from afar,
If you rub my snout,
Much good, without a doubt,
Will forever be yours.

# MONS ET MERVEILLES    **⑮**

9, rue du Costillon 83440 Mons
• Tel: 04 94 76 35 66
• Open daily except the days when it's closed ... but that's rarely the case!

### *The king of matches*

**A**t "Mons et Merveilles", the store's fabulous model boats made of (used) matches, built by Robert Audibert, never fail to impress.

It was 1948 that this boy, then 11 years old, acquired his lifelong passion for matches. He first built a chalet, which he still displays with some emotion, then a train, before going on to tackle boats. Today, after 58 years of leisure (as he puts it), he now enjoys an active retirement in his store/workshop, where he continues to plan and then carry out increasingly mad, audacious projects. All of his models are made with used matches that he recovers from all the people who save them for him. A little glue and the deed is done, or almost ... because for example, his model of *Hermione*, a frigate that is being reconstituted in full size at Rochefort, Robert Audibert spent nearly 1,720 hours working at a scale of 1/75, using 4,480 matches.

You can also admire his models of the *Astrolabe* – the ship of the French navigator *La Pérouse* – the aircraft carriers *Clemenceau* and *Jeanne d'Arc*, and the three caravels of Christopher Columbus, all of them crafted with amazing precision, especially taking into account the rather crude nature of the raw material employed.

But his indisputable masterpiece remains his very beautiful model of the village of Mons, displayed in his window day and night. And the most unusual piece must be his self-portrait, very striking indeed.

## SIGHTS NEARBY

### LA ROCHE TAILLÉE    **⑯**
### STARTING-POINT OF THE FRÉJUS AQUEDUCT
RD56 83440 Mons
• Access: from Mons, take the RD56 in the direction of Callian. La Roche Taillée is 8 km away, on the left of the road.

If the magnificent remnants of the Roman aqueduct running between Mons and Fréjus are well known, its starting-point is less familiar. Near the town of Mons, 40 km from Fréjus, the builders of the aqueduct overcame the natural obstacle of an immense mass of rock by creating a breach 50 m long, 3 m wide and 10 m high. The site is both spectacular and moving: the traces left by the tools wielded by human strength alone are still visible. In the central section of this "canal", a tunnel regulated the flow of water. The purpose of the aqueduct was to bring the water of the Siagnole River, whose source nearby, to Fréjus.

# WELLS OF THE HOLY VIRGIN

**17**

Chemin des Puits
06530 Saint-Cézaire-sur-Siagne

*Ancient Roman wells?*

**B**elow the village of Saint-Cézaire-sur-Siagne, a group of nine wells catches the eye. Four of them are covered by hemispherical vaults and were probably reserved for supplying water for human use, while the others, with low rims, surrounded by troughs, and equipped with hooks fixed in the stone, served to water animals. Previously known as "Roman wells" (although they were restored between the 16th and 18th centuries), the group was renamed as the "wells of the Holy Virgin" when a column dedicated to the Virgin Mary was built in 1865.

The wells are fed by groundwater that sometimes reaches as high as the grass on the surface, which would explain the number of wells, which were meant to "cover" the entire area of this upswelling. For this reason the group is inaccessible, although visible, as it is fenced off.

## SIGHTS NEARBY

### THE EPITAPH OF PROSPER MERLE

**18**

Vieux Cimetière de Peymeinade
Rue Louis-Jeaume 06530 Peymeinade

Near the rear right-hand corner of the old cemetery at Peymeinade lies the tomb of Prosper Merle. Upon a simple two-leaf slab, you can read the epitaph of this militant republican: "Goodbye, citizen, goodbye. Remember where a friend awaits you. And do not forget my final words: neither clergy nor emperor nor king. Long live the Republic. All religions are nothing but superstitious fanaticism which serve to exploit humankind; the only real God is the natural law of the infinite that has always existed and will go on existing forever. Here the republican Prosper Merle de Spéracèdes-la-Ravanelle sleeps the sleep of the just. Born 12 July 1838. Deceased 25 November 1920; a civil burial."

### A STATUETTE OF SAINT-ROCH

**19**

Place Gervais-Court 06530 Peymeinade

In place Gervais-Court, over the door of the village church, you can see a statuette of Saint-Roch in multicoloured plaster dating from the 20th century. The saint is represented with a pilgrim's staff [*bourdon*] in his right hand, while his left points to a plague bubo on his knee, indicating that he survived this killer disease. Sheltered in a niche protected by bars, this representation of the saint is fairly common in the south of France, where he was often called upon to provide protection from the numerous epidemics that decimated the region.

Opposite the church, the blind side of a pretty house is in fact an amazing *trompe-l'œil*.

# THE LITTLE WALL OF THE CONSCRIPTS

Corner of avenue Sidi-Brahim and rue Martine-Carol 06130 Grasse
• The wall is opposite Les Micocouliers bus stop and the tennis courts of the
Mercure hotel, in the recess that leads to a private dwelling.

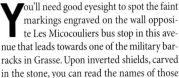

*Moving
testimonies
of men going
to war ...*

**Y**ou'll need good eyesight to spot the faint markings engraved on the wall opposite Les Micocouliers bus stop in this avenue that leads towards one of the military barracks in Grasse. Upon inverted shields, carved in the stone, you can read the names of those belonging to the same age group who wished to leave a trace of going into the army ... or off to war. A cross surmounted by a heart divides the shields into two columns. On one of the engravings appears a horn and a trumpet, as well as the names of those concerned, who, given the hardness of the stone, must have spent considerable time and effort on this work.

## SIGHTS NEARBY

### LA MAISON TOURNAIRE: A MONUMENTAL FAKE
Place de la Roque 06130 Grasse

Albert Tournaire, an architect from Nice and laureate of the Grand Prix of Rome, known as a practical joker, made a bet that he could get a false façade which he had stuck onto an 18th century house house listed as a 14th-century historical monument. He managed this feat as a decree dated 21 October 1932 validated the listing – erring by four centuries.

# THE *CANNE* AND THE DONJON

㉒

Place Francis-Paulet
06620 Le Bar-sur-Loup

> *The unit of length was engraved in the wall so that everybody could use it*

Seven storeys high, the base of the donjon of the chateau (now gone) stands in the main square of Le Bar-sur-Loup. Already mentioned in 971 by a document at Lérins Abbey, its upper storeys were destroyed during the Revolution in order to erase all traces of the ancien régime. If you look carefully, however, at the wall just to the left of the tourist office housed in the donjon, you will see a powerful symbol that escaped the revolutionary censors: a *canne*, a unit of measure in use prior to the adoption of the Republican metric system, is embedded in the surface.

In 1235, the counts of Le Bar seigneury were authorized to mint coins and establish their own system of measurements. In a feudal France where each lord regulated units of measurement according to his own interests, the cacophony of weights and measures was a real problem. The utility of presenting itinerant traders with the local standard was essential, and thus the *canne* of Le Bar was displayed so that everybody could refer to it.

The *canne* ranged between 1.71 m and 2.98 m within the kingdom of France but was around 1.98 m in Provence: 2.01 m in Marseille and 1.88 m in Nice, while that of Le Bar-sur-Loup measured 1.80 m.

## THE METRIC SYSTEM

It was on 1 August 1793 that the Convention adopted the metric system to replace the ancien régime's units of measurement. These, characterized by their archaic nature, were derived from local habits and customs handed down over millennia. Conversions from one set of measures to another were complex and completely lacking in any logic, so that any idea of basing a system on a "national", much less "European", unit was illusory, and was a handicap to trade. Measurements of distance, for example, could be made in points, pouces, lignes, toises, pied-de-roi, perche-du-roi or perche ordinaire, arpents and lieues (with ancient, Parisian and postal service variants …).

On 3 Messidor, year VII (22 June 1799), two standards made from platinum for the metre and the kilogram were deposited in the Archives (the French national records office). In 1875, the Conférence générale des Poids et Mesures (CGPM – General Conference on Weights and Measures) was set up, which finally renamed the decimal metric system as the Système International d'Unités (SI) in 1960.

# THE GIRLS' SCHOOL RESTAURANT ❷❸

380, avenue Amiral-de-Grasse 06620 Le Bar-sur-Loup
• Tel: 04 93 09 40 20
• Fax: 04 93 42 94 97
• E-mail: ecoledesfilles@wanadoo.fr
• www.restoecoledesfilles.fr

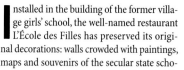

*A restaurant in a school*

Installed in the building of the former village girls' school, the well-named restaurant L'École des Filles has preserved its original decorations: walls crowded with paintings, maps and souvenirs of the secular state school. The proprietor will tell you all about the life of Célestin Freinet (see below) and serve you a light Provençal cuisine. The restaurant has been awarded the label *cuisine niçoise*: the *raviolis à la daube, farcis*, and *salade niçoise* are guaranteed to conform with tradition.

### SIGHTS NEARBY

#### THE SCHOOL OF CÉLESTIN FREINET ❷❹
Mairie
Place de la Tour 06620 Le Bar-sur-Loup

It was in the village school here that Célestin Freinet (1896-1966) began to experiment in the 1920's with the basic elements of his pedagogy: the Freinet method of education. His classroom is now a meeting room for the municipal council, and only a plaque next to the entrance of the mairie bears witness to his achievements.

#### THE FREINET METHOD

Célestin Freinet (1896–1966) experimented at the beginning of the 1920s in his school at Le Bar-sur-Loup (see above), with what would become the essence of his teaching methods. These favoured expression and communication, individual work, autonomy, experimental trial-and-error, the cooperative organization of classes (each member finding a role to play), as well as a more responsibility for the pupil. He rejected the school textbook and "brainwashing", publicized his initiatives in the press, and built up a network of correspondents. His school was organized as a real community and the children called the Freinet couple *papa* and *maman*. Practical activities, participation in drawing up timetables, and editiong a class newspaper were just some of the innovations called for by his method. Freinet is remembered in particular for the following principle: "Democracy in school prepares the democracy of tomorrow." For more information, see the website: www.icem-freinet.info. Célestin Freinet also taught at Saint-Paul-de-Vence and at Vence, where he set up his own private school.

## THE SALT CHAIR IN THE MUSÉE HISTORIQUE

Château de Gourdon 06620 Gourdon
• Tel: 04 93 09 68 02 • Fax: 04 93 09 68 97
• E-mail: chateaudegourdon@hotmail.com • www.château-gourdon.com
• Opening hours: June to September, 11.00–13.00 and 14.00–19.00; October to May, 14.00–18.00, except Tuesday.

> *Proof of the inventiveness of salt tax evaders*

Famed for its beauty, its "balcony" location overlooking the Gorges du Loup, its gardens, and its two museums, the Château de Gourdon has some astonishing pieces in its historical museum.

The salt chair, in which grandmother was often found seated, allowed families to hide away salt from the eyes of the *gabelou*, the customs officer charged with catching evaders of the salt tax. Placed near the fireplace, it also kept the salt dry.

Among the well-known original paintings displayed in the museum is the remarkable triptych by Barent Van Orley with its right-hand panel entitled *The Circumcision*, a subject which the Roman Catholic Church has apparently considered best left forgotten, since the feast of the Saint-Prépuce [Holy Foreskin], which used to be celebrated on 1 January, was quietly dropped from the religious calendar in 1970.

Another outstanding painting is a panel portraying the legend of Saint Ursula, which represents the saint with 11,000 virgins. This legend seems to stem from an error in interpretation: her hand in marriage having been demanded by a pagan German prince, Ursula, wishing to remain a virgin and a Christian, fled with ten female friends who were also virgins. Washed up on the banks of the Rhine by a storm, they were captured by the Huns, tortured and put to death when they refused to betray their faith. When an engraved stone referring to this story was found in 1155, the figure "XIMV" was interpreted as fixing the number of virgins accompanying Ursula at 11,000, instead of 11 for "XI", the "M" being the abbreviation for martyrs and the "V" for virgins.

### THE *GABELLE*

Derived from the Arabic *kabala* which means "tax", the word *gabelle* was applied to the tax on salt in Franche-Comté starting in the 14th century, the king being considered the owner of the ground and its products. Over the next four and a half centuries, and particularly after the increases in salt prices imposed by the French chief minister Colbert in the 17th century, the *gabelle* became one of the most unpopular taxes in France. Despite the sanctions against the *faux-sauniers* [salt smugglers] – years in the galleys and even the death sentence – the French people used every means at their disposal to evade the salt tax. As the clergy, the nobility, royal officers and members of the University all benefited from a major reduction, it is thought that the *gabelle* was one of the factors that helped to stir up revolution in the country. The tax was finally abolished by the Constituent Assembly in 1790.

# IN AND AROUND SAINT-TROPEZ

# TEMPLE OF HERCULES, CAVALIÈRE

Rue du Temple, Cavalière, 83980 Le Lavandou
• Access to the temple, although not prohibited, is totally inadvisable for safety reasons and because it stands on private property. For a close view, turn left at the roundabout at the entrance to Cavalière onto boulevard de l'Hubac-du-Bleu, which becomes chemin de l'Hubac-du-Bleu, then left onto rue du Temple. From the end of this impasse, in the Hubac du Bleu estate, you can best see the temple. Coming back down, a road cuts across on the left, also a dead end. From there the road is closed by a red and white barrier for fire service access. The road goes below the temple, but don't take it: it is too complicated and dangerous to go any further.

> *A rare neoclassical construction*

lthough from a distance Lavandou's Temple of Hercules seems authentic, in fact it only dates from the early 20th century.

At that time Arthur Engelfred, engineer, art and archaeology enthusiast, undertook a dig at Cavalière looking for traces of the ancient city of Alconis, a Greek trading post that was part of the colony of Marseille. He discovered the foundations of a small antique temple, on which he decided to set up a museum in the style of a Greek temple to house his archaeological finds. An artist whom we have unfortunately been unable to identify, winner of the Prix de Rome (French scholarship for art students), supplied the two caryatids that adorn the structure, a more or less faithful copy of the famous treasury of Sifnos built on Delphi in 525 BC.

While the museum was still open to visitors, it was said that beside artefacts from Engelfred's digs you could see a magic lantern that projected scenes from antiquity onto the walls, a tearoom, and Omphale's stone, whose hidden navel would increase by ten years the life expectancy of anyone finding it.

Today the temple is falling into ruin and no restoration project is planned. At Lavandou, where clearly everything is counted in twelves (the 12 sands of 12 beaches, 12 fountains), why not launch a theme on the "12 labours of Hercules"?

## SIGHTS NEARBY

### CHAPELLE NOTRE-DAME-DE-CONSTANCE
Col de Caguo-Ven, D41, 83230 Bormes-les-Mimosas
• Open daily 15.00–18.00 • Access by two footpaths: one leaves from the chateau and is lined with oratories, the other 1 km from the village on the way to Collobrières (small car park and sign indicating the chapel). Either route will take about half an hour's walk.

Above the very beautiful village of Bormes-les-Mimosas, among the pines and outcrops of schist, Notre-Dame-de-Constance chapel is still a popular place of pilgrimage; in the notebooks set out for the pilgrims they write vows to the Virgin, such as a prettily drawn Star of David with the mention "Thank you for having accepted me", which gives a good idea of the ecumenical impression given by this place. Although some messages are poignant, they all bear the traces of the sincerity of those who have climbed up the hill to come here, perhaps closer to heaven, to write to the Virgin Mary. Thanks are due to the Association Sauvegarde Vieux-Bormes, which has made possible the chapel restoration.

# THE CABIN OF CHATEAU DE VALMER

Hôtel-Restaurant Château de Valmer, Gigaro, 83420 La Croix-Valmer
• Tel: 04 94 55 15 15 • Fax: 04 94 55 15 10
• www.chateauvalmer.com • E-mail: info@chateauvalmer.com
• Cabin rates: €320—400 depending on season

*A luxury
hotel room
in a tree*

N ear the village of Croix-Valmer, on the Saint-Tropez peninsula, the luxury hotel-restaurant of Château de Valmer is housed in the former country mansion of a 19th-century wine-growing domain. The hotel brochure speaks for itself through a couple of dozen well-chosen photographs. Other than the 42 rooms within the hotel, three residences are available, the Cabanon, the Mas provençal and above all, the superb Cabane perchée.

This last tree house, set in an immense 100-year-old oak, is a little way from the hotel and so lets you take full advantage of the calm countryside and the surrounding vineyard. The made-to-measure cabin follows the shape of the tree, allowing its branches to grow around the terrace. The interior design, comfortably rustic, is equipped with all the features you would expect in a luxury hotel. On the terrace the garden furniture and loungers invite rest, calm and peace.

### A CROSS IN THE SKY
The cross of Col de la Croix, Carrefour des Feux
Junction of D559 and D93, 83420 La Croix-Valmer

The name of the village of Croix-Valmer comes from a historic episode of which the cross set in a little square at the so-called Col de la Croix is a reminder. In AD 312, the Roman emperor Constantine I left Arles to go into battle against his rival Maxentius, who had had himself proclaimed emperor of Rome. On the way, Constantine's army set up a temporary camp at the site of Croix-Valmer. It was there that he saw a vision in the sky of a cross accompanied by these words: *In hoc signo vinces* (In this sign, you will conquer). Impressed by this divine demonstration, Constantine immediately converted to Christianity, convinced that the sign was a premonition of his victory over Maxentius, which finally took place at the Battle of the Milvian Bridge, on the outskirts of Rome.

At the very spot where this vision is supposed to have occurred, the cross was erected in 1893. La Croix-Valmer has moreover adopted the enigmatic phrase written in the sky as the commune's motto.

Historians now think that the anecdote is too good to be true and that Constantine only converted to Christianity afterwards.

# MUSÉE DU COQ

Demeure-Musée Sellier
46, rue Nationale, 83310 Cogolin
• Tel: 04 94 54 63 28 • E-mail: info@cogolin-provence.com
• Open Tuesday to Saturday, from 1 June to 30 September 10.00–13.00 and
15.00–18.30, from 1 October to 31 May 10.00–12.30 and 14.30–17.30
• Admission: €2.30 • Students and under-16s free

*From coq au lin to Cogolin*

The Cockerel Museum is, as its name indicates, devoted to the fowl, presented here in the most diverse forms and materials (pottery, wrought iron, glass, bronze, tin, wood). After the first room with its rare four-legged cockerel (stuffed), there are worldwide examples of this farmyard favourite and its use in politics, advertising and sport.

There's nothing strange in the fact that this museum is to be found at Cogolin, as the town owes its name to a famous bird: when a Roman officer under Nero, Torpeus, was beheaded in AD 68 for refusing to deny his Christian faith, his body was placed in a barge at the mouth of the River Arno (Italy) with a cock and a dog on board. When the barge ran aground on the shores of what would become Saint-Tropez, the cock flew off and alighted in a field of *lin* [flax, for making linen] which would become Cogolin, a corruption of *coq-au-lin* if you'd like to believe the legend …

The identification of the cockerel with France comes from the Latin word *gallus*, which means both "cock" and "Gaul". Although the cock appeared as a national symbol during the Revolution, it became an official emblem in the reign of Louis-Philippe, in 1830, and came to the fore particularly strongly during the First World War, in opposition to the Prussian eagle. Although the bird emblem is has now officially been replaced by Marianne, it retains a strong hold on the public imagination.

## SIGHTS NEARBY

### MEDIEVAL AND TEMPLARS' MUSEUM, COGOLIN

Entry included in the ticket for the *demeure-musée* Sellier.

On the upper floor of the Sellier mansion, two rooms filled with life-size figures in rich costumes are devoted to the Templars. Some 200 information panels and a number of models tell you all you ever wanted to know about this military religious order with a sinister reputation. The Association Empreintes et Traditions du pays des Maures et de Provence is responsible for this permanent exhibition notable for its seriousness, quality of documentation and informative approach.

## LE MUSÉE RAIMU ❻

18, avenue Georges-Clemenceau, 83310 Cogolin
- Tel: 04 94 54 18 00 • Fax: 04 94 54 43 24 • www.musee-raimu.com
- Open daily 10.00–12.00 and 15.00–18.00 (off-season), 10.00–12.00 and 16.00–19.00 (high season)
- Closed Sunday morning and Tuesdays except during school vacations
- Admission: €3.50 • Children over 11: €1.75

### "I wanted to meet the greatest actor who ever lived"

When Orson Welles asked to meet Raimu, it was too late – he had died a few days earlier. The celebrated American film-maker and actor came out with the disappointed remark: "I wanted to meet the greatest actor who ever lived."

Visiting the Musée Raimu today is to recapture the ambiance and personality of this extraordinary actor who retains his fascination, not only in the roles he played for Marcel Pagnol but also in many films enshrined in the history of the cinema.

The museum, run by the actor's grand-daughter Isabelle Nohain, displays souvenirs of his early days (before Jules Muraire, his real name, was changed to Raimu), original film posters, over 200 photos of his times, scripts and contracts, a selection of costumes, souvenirs of *Marius* and *La Femme du boulanger* [*The Baker's Wife*] and the ubiquitous hat with the symbolic overcoat

from his last film *L'homme au chapeau rond* [*The Eternal Husband*].

Upstairs, a more private section shows personal belongings and clothing (Raimu was extremely elegant), some of the furnishings from his Bandol house and his Parisian apartment in rue de Washington.

On a wall is a pleasing nod to Raimu from comic books: plates from the four Asterix albums he directed for the cinema: *Le tour de Gaule d'Astérix*, *La Serpe d'or*, *Astérix et le chaudron* and *Astérix en Corse* [*Asterix and the Banquet*, *Asterix and the Golden Sickle*, *Asterix and the Cauldron* and *Asterix in Corsica*].

# LE FORT FREINET

Le fort Freinet, 83680 La Garde-Freinet

• Access: there are two ways of getting to Fort Freinet. For both you'll need strong footwear. For the first, drive out of the village on the RD558 towards Grimaud. Take the street that leads up to the right after the bowling ground until you reach a car park. A path takes you to the cross in 10 minutes. From there, follow the yellow markers to the fort. Alternatively, park at Aire de la Planète north of the village, and take the path which, after several metres, splits into two. The left branch leads to the cross, and straight on leads to the fort. At the next fork, turn left up the path. It will take about 25 minutes to reach the fort from there. Although it is theoretically possible to then make the detour back to the cross from the fort, the path is thought to be difficult for anyone prone to vertigo.

> ## *The Saracens at Saint-Tropez*

Gouged from the rock to a depth of 8 m, the defensive ditches of La Garde-Freinet fort are an impressive sight. The panorama is breathtaking and, from a strategic point of view, it is easy to understand why this eagle's nest dominating the region, from the Rock of Roquebrune to Les Maures, from Luc to Le Muy, from the sea to the foothills of the Alps, attracted the Saracens.

A number of historians, including at least four Arabs, have identified La Garde-Freinet with the ancient Fraxinet, founded around AD 880 by a couple of dozen Saracens whose boat capsized in the Gulf of Saint-Tropez. Assisted by reinforcements from Andalusia, the holders of the citadel used it as a base from which to launch attacks on local ports and towns. This is thought to be how Fréjus and Toulon came to be burned and pillaged, although some archaeologists have now cast doubt on this hypothesis.

It was only thanks to a great collaborative effort between, among others, Guillaume of Provence, the Counts of Forcalquier and of Turin, as well as the Viscount of Marseille, that the Saracen occupation was ended in 973. Six centuries later, the Maréchal de Valletta finally had the fort destroyed so that members of the Sainte Ligue [Holy League] couldn't use it as a refuge.

Today, other than the ditches, you can see the remains of a chapel, an oven, the chateau and some 40 huts.

## SIGHTS NEARBY

### CROSS OF THE MOORS: "CHRIST BEFORE YOU"

6 m high and standing on one of the paths leading to the fort, the "Cross of the Moors" was erected in 1900 in place Neuve opposite the most imposing house in the village (now the tourist office), whose owner was known for his anti-clerical opinions. The priest of the time, the man behind it all, is said to have shouted to the impious one: "Until the end of your days, you will have Christ before you!"

### MOORS AND SARACENS

The Moors were Berber nomads living in the region of what is now Morocco in the 6th century BC. After their Romanization and Christianization, they converted to Islam in the 8th century and occupied Spain until 1492.

The word Saracen has been used to describe, since medieval times and the Crusades, peoples of the Muslim faith.

# LE CERCLE DU LITTORAL ⑨

Place Gabriel-Péri, 83350 Ramatuelle • Tel: 04 94 79 26 74
• Private association • Subscription: €10 per year (with the agreement of the commission and sponsorship of two members)
• You can also visit the circle by invitation from a member. Try to find someone who'll invite you on the spot and have some refreshments while you're waiting.

> **"Entering the circle, I leave outside everything that separates us and I preciously conserve all that unites us"**

Founded in 1885, the Cercle du Littoral is the oldest local association. Its aim: "to create a meeting of men (women being excluded at the time) of good company, desirous of seeing one another and entertaining themselves either by conversation, reading a variety of newspapers, brochures and books (and by card parties …)". An additional benefit of the circle is worth having: refreshments are much cheaper because the association is non-profit.

After the Revolution, a number of these circles grew up in Provence. First there were "bourgeois" or "white" circles, so-called because that social class had discovered the freedom of expression and could apply themselves to a really French passion: discussing politics!

Later, "red" circles were set up with, as you might expect, ideas very much more to the left.

At Ramatuelle, associations representing each of the two distinct social strata decided to join together and run a single circle, which was given the neutral name "Cercle du Littoral" (Circle of the Coast). Hence its motto, which means: "Entering the circle, I leave outside everything that separates us and I preciously conserve all that unites us." Today there are only 26 circles left in the Var *département* from over 300 that existed at the end of the 19th century.

## SIGHTS NEARBY ⑩

Inside the village church, to the left under a vault, there are three framed tributes to the crew of three submarines (*Eurydice, Minerve* and *Sibylle*), which came to land or pick up secret agents from the beach at Escalet (see opposite site).

### ANDROUNO DE GASSIN : THE NARROWEST STREET IN THE WORLD?

You'll never tire of strolling round the village of Gassin with its streets, passageways, tiny squares and tastefully restored houses. Everything is fine until you reach the Androuno, a street (if it can be called one) that passes (!) for the narrowest in the world, although this record hasn't yet been validated by Guinness World Records. Admittedly, if you're on the heavy side, it would be risky to try: the distance between the two walls is no more than 29 cm in places. The name *androuno* comes from the Greek *andros* (man) and *uno* (one), implying that you can only pass along the street one at a time.

# MONUMENT TO THE SERVICES SPÉCIAUX

Square Alfasser, 83350 Ramatuelle

> *Homage to secret agents*

**A**t Ramatuelle, an eminently touristic commune on the Saint-Tropez peninsula, an amazing monument is dedicated to the memory of around 300 secret agents who fought the enemy during the Second World War. Its official title commands respect: *Mémorial des anciens des services spéciaux de la Défense Nationale (ASSDN)*.

The choice of the site of Ramatuelle was natural enough because it was in a nearby *calanque* [rocky inlet] that many of the secret agents were landed from Free French submarines (*Le Casabianca, L'Aréthuse, Le Marsouin, La Perle*). Moreover, a good many Ramatuelle residents formed part of the local Resistance, which helped the undercover agents to fulfil their dangerous missions in occupied territory.

The names of these shadowy agents can be seen today in Alsfasser Square (named after Alphonse Alfasser, a "chief of mission" killed at Ramatuelle, where he is buried), engraved on the marble monument. Designed by the architect Gaston Castel, it was sculpted by Marcel Courbier, a friend of the French Resistance hero Jean Moulin.

## GASTON CASTEL

Gaston Castel was born in Pertuis on 1 August 1886 and died on 9 February 1971 at Marseille. From a family of stonemasons, he was accepted by the Marseille School of Architecture and received the Grand Prix de Rome in 1913. He was disfigured during World War I and had to undergo a bone graft, which failed to give the hoped-for result but left him minus an eye. He thus became a one-eyed architect ... Later, he went to Rio to work on the Brazilian independence monument with his sculptor friend Antoine Sartorio. At Marseille, he built the Opéra, the Monument aux Héros de l'Armée d'Orient and Les Baumettes prison, decorated with low reliefs of the seven cardinal sins (see the guidebook in this series, *Marseille insolite et secret*). After the Second World War, he took part in the reconstruction of the Vieux-Port of Marseille (1945–1953) with Fernand Pouillon. His house in Marseille (2, rue Croix-de-Régnier), listed as a historic monument, is now being restored and part of it is used as a guest house (see the above-mentioned guide).

## THE MARIANNE OF SAINT-TROPEZ TOWN HALL

Mairie de Saint-Tropez
Place de l'Hôtel-de-Ville
83990 Saint-Tropez
• At Saint-Tropez town hall, go to the reception. If no weeding ceremony is taking place, you can visit the *salle des mariages* • Photos are allow.

> **To be sure of meeting BB**

I t is sometimes said that Brigitte Bardot has made Saint-Tropez the most fashionable Mediterranean port since the 1960s. However many tourists have tried to approach La Madrague, the star's house by the shore, it's rare for any to catch a glimpse of her. To be sure of meeting her, all you have to do is visit the salle des mariages in the town hall where, in a niche above the mayor's chair, Marianne wears the features of the woman long known as "BB". You'll notice that for a national symbol, the bust shown there is rather sensuous …

### MARIANNE

In the guise of a woman wearing a Phrygian cap [the red cap of liberty], Marianne is the allegorical figure of the French Republic and represents the enduring values of the republic and of French citizens: "Liberty, Equality, Fraternity".

The name Marianne seems to have come from a contraction of Marie and Anne, two very common forenames in the 18th century among the female subjects of the French kingdom. It was a certain Guillaume Lavabre who, in October 1792, for the first time baptized the Republic "Marianne" in a hugely popular song, *La Garisou de Marianno* [The healing of Marianne]. Since the 1970s, film stars or singers, and recently television personalities, have served as models for Marianne: Brigitte Bardot in 1970, Mireille Mathieu in 1978, Catherine Deneuve in 1985, Laetitia Casta in 2000 and Evelyne Thomas in 2003.

### SIGHTS NEARBY

#### ZANZIBAR DOOR

Unmissable – although everybody knows about it, this door is still one of the most unusual curiosities of the town. Mozarab in style, it was brought back from his long voyages by a Saint-Tropez ship's captain whose family had opened the first French trading post in Madagascar. He brought it from the island of Zanzibar to embellish his family home.

## THE BAR OF HÔTEL SUBE ⓮

15, quai de Suffren, 83990 Saint-Tropez
• Tel: 04 94 97 30 04 • Fax: 04 94 54 89 08
• E-mail: hotel-sube@wanadoo.fr • www.hotel-sube.com

*A harbour bar, far from the crowds*

You won't stumble upon the bar of Hôtel Sube. Only the hotel residents and the regulars know the way from the port of Saint-Tropez to the quai de Suffren, just behind the statue of the eponymous bailiff. To the right, on the first floor, an automatic door opens onto paradise (even though the name Sube makes is rather reminiscent of a submarine hotel …)

Starting from the reception desk, the atmosphere of this place, unique to Saint-Tropez, fills you with a sense of well-being. The place has the looks and

style of a real English club, with its pictures and posters on the walls, its magnificent bar, its model boats and its view of the part. Ensconced in the leather armchairs, deep and burnished, you savour, especially in the high season, the incomparable and delectable feeling of being lucky to have enough escaped from the flood of holidaymakers in shorts and sandals gazing at the stars, or wannabes, on the decks of the yachts.

Off-season, the ambiance is just as pleasant because, in winter, local people and all manner of seamen gather around the bar's fireplace. The Sube, the oldest hotel in Saint-Tropez still operating, is also second home (after Paris) to the Yacht Club de France, whose flag flies on the balcony.

### SIGHTS NEARBY

#### STATUE OF THE BAILIFF OF SUFFREN ⓯

Hôtel Sube is just behind the statue of the bailiff of Suffren, a typical Saint-Tropez character. Although the bronze is majestic, it doesn't quite match up with the unsightly physical reality of this man. Born at Saint-Cannat (near Aix-en-Provence) in 1729, he attained the rank of lieutenant-general in the navy, then vice-admiral of France. In 1775, the king nominated him "Lieutenant du Roy de la ville de Saint-Tropez et Gouverneur de sa Citadelle". The statue, presented to the town by Napoleon III, was cast from the bronze of the cannons taken from the hereditary enemy of the time: the English.

## SAINT-TROPEZ AND SAINTE-MAXIME

Why is there no clock on the fourth face of the tower of Notre-Dame-de-l'Assomption church, which stands empty? Gossips say that the reason is to stop the people of Sainte-Maxime reading the time from the Saint-Tropez clock. However, residents of that town on the other side of the gulf would have to have good eyesight – or good binoculars – to put their trust in Saint-Tropez time! What's more, the Saint-Tropez folk will tell you that the Sainte-Maxime folk are the happiest in the world because they can see Saint-Tropez all day long!

## SIGHTS NEARBY

### THE TWIN HOUSES OF SAINTE-MAXIME 16
18 and 20, place Louis-Blanc, 83120 Sainte-Maxime

Built at the end of the 19th century, these twin houses have a pleasing history: the two business partners who had them built didn't know how best to allocate them because of the different amount of land that went with each house. So they decided to draw lots on the day of completion, which explains why they are so very similar …

### THE ELEPHANTS' BEACH: LA PLAGE DE BABAR 17
RN98 , 83120 Sainte-Maxime

East of Sainte-Maxime is a resort called Elephants' Beach. For those who are curious to know the origin of this name, we can only suggest that they open a copy of the children's book

*Le Voyage de Babar.* On page 4 or 5, depending on the edition, Babar and Céleste on honeymoon fly over a beautiful Mediterranean beach, the very one that bears the name Elephants' Beach and for that very reason.

The explanation is simply that the creator of Babar, Jean de Brunhoff, lived at Sainte-Maxime and was inspired to include this beach in the second volume of his worldwide success …

Virtual tour of Elephants' Beach: www.ste-maxime.com

# LE MUSÉE DU PHONOGRAPHE  ⓲

Parc de Saint-Donat, CD25, 83120 Sainte-Maxime
- Tel: 04 94 96 50 52 • Fax: 04 94 47 02 64
- E-mail: musee.phono@infonie.fr
- Guided tour of 1 hour can be booked
- Adults: €3 • Children from 6 to 16: €1.50
- Access: 10 km from Sainte-Maxime on Le Muy road. At Saint-Donnat turn right onto a rough track that leads to the museum, 300 m from the road. Be careful as the signposting is rudimentary, where it exists at all

> ### *From music box to ... music box*

The eclectic and fanciful frontage of the Gramophone Museum is an astonishing creation. Although the interior is just a vast space where hundreds of more or less unique pieces are stored without any special attempt to display them to advantage, the guided tour is captivating.

It begins with the first mechanical pianos worked by perforated strips, ancestors of the modern computer. Note that all the machines on show are in working order and the guide will demonstrate them, thus inviting you to share in a very pleasant musical tour.

There is one surprise after another as you look round: the first paying jukebox with a time lag (the coins feeding the machine fall only after a certain time, so as never to interrupt a record), the first sound recorder consisting of a glass ball with a bevelled edge, as well as horn gramophones, cylinder gramophones and finally record players. The museum possesses a few pieces that are exceptional as much for their aesthetic as their practical value, some now obsolete like the first dictaphone dating from 1903, with its microphone for the boss and headphone for the typist.

The other interesting aspect of the museum is the fact that the field of sound reproduction comes into perspective once and for all with all these inventions that have changed the daily life of humanity.

# THE GALLO-ROMAN TANK OF ISSAMBRES

Sentier du Littoral, RN98 , 83380 Les Issambres

• Access: the fish tank is about 1 km south of Pointe de la Tourterelle and very easy to find as it's signposted at the roadside (Corniche des Maures). You can leave your vehicle in the car park and then follow the coastal footpath for a short distance; the tank is just beside the path.

*Running water fish tank from antiquity*

Listed as a historical monument since 1939, the Issambres tank is the only existing example from ancient Gaul with running water and in a good state of repair. It shows the interest that the local property owners already had for fresh fish. The tank had two functions: capturing the fish and keeping them alive in their natural environment.

Above the tank a panel explains in very clear diagrams how this fish reserve works. In the first place, you have to catch the fish. Sometimes a male fish was used, held captive by a line and pulled towards the trap when the females decided to follow him. Then, as soon as the fish had entered the ponds, they were shut in. The three ponds, of different depth and size, were separated by man-made walls and their water was regularly renewed by a system of channels and gates. A walkway allowed workers to move around the edges of the tank.

Archaeologists think that this tank was attached to a Gallo-Roman villa discovered nearby, in the Gaillarde inlet. In one of the rooms, a mosaic was found with a medallion showing a dolphin swimming between two tridents.

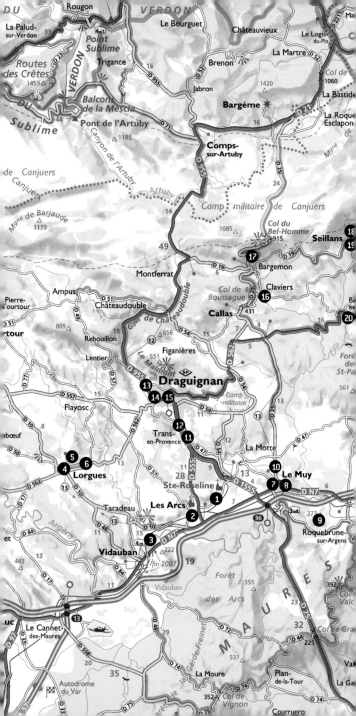

# IN AND AROUND DRAGUIGNAN

# THE RELIQUARY OF SAINT ROSELINE'S EYES

Chapelle Sainte Roseline
D91
83460 Les Arcs-sur-Argens
• Open Tuesday to Sunday 14.30 to 18.30 in summer and 14.00–17.00 in winter
• Pilgrimages Trinity Sunday (the first after Pentecost), the first Sunday in August, the Sunday before Palm Sunday and the nearest Sunday to 16 October.

> **The miraculous power of St Roseline's eyes**

Stored in a *châsse\** inside the chapel that bears her name, between the villages of Les Arcs and Trans, St Roseline has been the source of a number of miracles.

Daughter of Sybille de Sabran and d'Arnaud de Villeneuve, Roseline lived in the 14th century and was known for her generosity. While her father was opposed to her dishing out charity, Roseline was in the habit of distributing the chateau's stores to those who had nothing to eat. One day, however, her father surprised her with a full apron, which he suspected contained foodstuffs but, to his stupefaction, roses miraculously flew out of it.

At her death, her body, displayed in a *châsse*, was miraculously preserved. It was nevertheless lost during the Wars of Religion but later recovered … by a blind man. Pilgrims were staggered by her shining eyes, which seemed to be as vital as before her death. The tale even reached the ears of Louis XIV, who attempted to find out if this was trickery and sent his physician Vallot to make an incision in the saint's eye. Her eyes then closed for ever.

Now enclosed in a reliquary separate from the châsse, her eyes still keep their miraculous powers, as borne out by the vast amount of ex-votos and the many pilgrimages that still take place today.

Several years ago, Marguerite Maeght obtained permission for eminent artists to come and create pieces to help towards the restoration of the chapel, now richly endowed with contemporary work. You can also see there windows by Bazaine and Ubac and bronzes by Diego Giacometti, brother of Alberto (a lectern, the doors of the reliquary). An immense mosaic by Marc Chagall also represents an episode from the life of St Roseline: when she was a novice at Bertaud Abbey, she forgot to prepare the meals she was responsible for. Her duties were taken over by angels, who appeared to do the cooking and serving in her place.

[\*] *Châsse*: glass reliquary or shrine in which the relics of a saint may be seen.

# CHÂTEAU FONT DU BROC

83460 Les Arcs-sur-Argens
- Tel. 04 94 47 48 20 • Fax: 04 94 47 50 46
- E-mail: caveau@chateau-fontdubroc.com • www.chateau-fontdubroc.com
- Open from Monday to Saturday 9.00–12.00 and 14.00–18.00, Sunday 14.00–18.00

> *Reproduction of the chapter house of Thoronet Abbey*

Font du Broc chateau was built on virgin ground in the late 1970s, despite its outward appearance. Sylvain Massa wanted to bring the 100 hectares of land, which had run to scrub, back to viticulture. The main interest of the site is the cellar where wine casks and bottles are stored – a faithful reproduction of the chapter house of nearby Thoronet Abbey. It is reached by a vertiginous stairway that leads to a subterranean cathedral, 20 m deep, which required four years of work. Very impressive with its abbey-like proportions, the cellar naturally maintains a constant temperature between 14 and 15 degrees. The construction was carried out by the Compagnons du Tour de France* and you have to admire the stone-cutting, the vaulting, the quality of the sculptures and the allusion to the "companions" in the form of a salamander [the symbolic masterpiece crafted by one of them] clinging to an archway.

A few days after the opening, however, part of the cellar vaulting collapsed but, miraculously, nobody was hurt.

The tour includes the ring where magnificent Lusitanian horses are trained, as well as the reception rooms, including the "biggest in the Var", as the brochure claims. Note that these sumptuous function and banqueting rooms are booked up a year in advance …

*The Compagnons du Tour de France are not part of the annual cycling epic but an organization of craftsmen and artisans dating from the Middle Ages and still active today. Their traditional educational techniques include touring France and taking up apprenticeships with masters of various trades.

## SIGHTS NEARBY

### UNE BORNE D'OCTROI
Route d'Italie 83550 Vidauban

The route d'Italie, a paved road leading to the hamlet of Blaïs, joins the RN7 on the left, 4 km from Vidauban, coming from Cannet-des-Maures. A toll boundary stone forms part of the wall, at the junction of chemin d'Italie and chemin de Barueti. You can clearly read the words "*octroi*" and "Vidauban".
The *octroi* was an indirect tax that communes used to impose on goods brought in to their area. Rabbits, eggs, fruit and vegetables, were all taxed and people often tried to hide what they were transporting. The office responsible for collecting the tax (which was also known as the *octroi*) controlled the city gates or the boundaries of a commune. This tax was abolished in France as recently as 1948.

# CHAPELLE NOTRE-DAME-DE-BENVA

D50

Route de Saint-Antonin 83510 Lorgues
• Open Thursdays in July and August, 10.00–12.00 and 15.00–17.00
• Group visits can be booked at Lorgues tourist office
Place Trussy 83510 Lorgues
• Tel. 04 94 73 92 37 • E-mail: lorotsi@aol.com

> **The invention of Purgatory**

**A** pearl of the Var heritage, the exterior of the chapel of Notre-Dame-de-Benva is unique in its architectural style, designed to encompass the medieval path that passed through the porch of the chapel. *Benva*, meaning *bon voyage*, goes wonderfully with the roadside location.

The well-deserved reputation of the chapel is especially due to its exceptional frescoes, dating from 1511. One of them represents purgatory in the form of a vast barred cell, in which hundreds of naked bodies are piled up, apparently being grilled (smoke is rising above them). Two angels, pitchers in hand, attempt unconvincingly to relieve their suffering.

Purgatory is a concept that the Church only accepted in the 13th century. It was at the fourth Council of Latran in 1215 that this intermediate state between death and Heaven was taken into Roman Catholic doctrine. This relatively punitive "interval" thus allowed venial sins committed during one's time on earth to be "purged". Purgatory became an extremely efficient source of funds: a believer could provide for "indulgences", gifts to the abbeys and other religious institutions to say a mass on their behalf, which would shorten their painful stay in Purgatory.

## INDULGENCES

The indulgence is a total or partial remission before God of temporal punishment due for having committed a sin. It is gained in part by an act of devotion (pilgrimage, prayer, mortification) carried out in the sacrament of penance. Simony [the buying or selling of privileges] is a perversion of the indulgence: believers sold to the priest a charitable act, which often became a gift in hard cash ...

A famous example dates from 1515, in which year the German Dominican friar Johann Tetzel was responsible for the sale of indulgences in the name of the archbishop of Mainz, Albert of Brandenburg, who kept back 50% of the proceeds to cover his living expenses. The height of cynicism, the slogan of the tax-collector monk who beat a drum to attract the crowds was "As soon as the coins clink in the trunk, the soul flies out of Purgatory". Martin Luther intervened in this scandalous state of affairs on 31 October 1517, Hallow'een (eve of All Saints' Day), posting his Ninety-five Theses denouncing the practice of granting indulgences. This episode is considered to be the "public launch" of the Reformation.

# MUSÉE PICTURAL ET ARCHITECTURAL ROB JULLIEN ❺

Le Moulin Rue Tré-Barry 83510 Lorgues
• Booking, information: 06 22 88 37 66
• Open 15.00–19.00 except Monday and Tuesday • Groups by arrangement
• Admission €4; children, groups €2

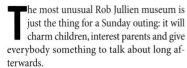

The most unusual Rob Jullien museum is just the thing for a Sunday outing: it will charm children, interest parents and give everybody something to talk about long afterwards.

> *A museum where the esoteric rules*

Rob Jullien, born in Aix-en-Provence, after spending some time in Paris fell in love with the former mill of Lorgues which he spent several years restoring, extending and decorating. He created the museum that bears his name, built in a style that is an esoteric reconstitution strongly inspired by the religious military order of the Templars, consisting of narrow and winding tunnels, sombre corridors and steep stairways. The Salle de la Chouette [Owl Room], with the tomb of what is thought to be a Templar, thus features a cleverly displayed Templar's cross. The artist's illustrative work is also on show: ranging from fantasy to science fiction, crystals and minerals, sometimes close to film posters.

### CROIX PATTÉE

The arms of the *croix pattée* or Templars' cross broaden from the centre and have indented ends, hence the name. This cross was the symbol of the Crusades and the colour red is the insignia of the Knights Templar.

## SIGHTS NEARBY

### A RARE POLITICAL EX-VOTO AT THE SANCTUARY OF SAINT-FERRÉOL ❻
Colline Saint-Férréol 83510 Lorgues
• Group tours only by arrangement • Association des Amis de Saint-Ferréol et du Vieux Lorgues • Contact: M. Delseray at 04 94 73 26 85

For many years, the Association des Amis de Saint-Ferréol et du Vieux Lorgues have done an impressive job in preserving and giving prominence to the exceptional religious heritage of the village. The Musée d'Art Sacré of Saint-Ferréol chapel thus offers a collection of ex-votos in perfect condition, some of which go back to the 17th century, as well as a strange piece of furniture containing a torn boot of beige leather, a rifle butt and a man's black garments riddled with bullet holes. The text inscribed below gives a clue: "In memory of 10 December 1851. Andéol de Rasque de Laval." This young man of 26, from a noble family, was taken hostage by Republianc insurgents who were responding to the coup d'état of Louis-Napoléon Bonaparte (the future Napoleon III) of 2 December 1851. He was wounded by the regular troops that came to suppress the uprising and owed his survival only to the intervention of an officer who noticed their mistake.

# VAROIS MUSEUM OF SCOUTING

40, boulevard Palayson
Lotissement Les Hauts de Palayson 83490 Le Muy
• Open Wednesday 14.00–17.00 and by arrangement • Tel. 04 94 45 84 83
• Admission free • Access: leave the village of Le Muy by the RN7, direction Fréjus. Carry on for 500 m after the Saint-Romain wine cooperative. At the shopping centre next to the "Incroyable" salerooms, turn left towards the entrance to two parallel routes separated by a bus shelter. Take the one that goes up to the left, signposted "Les Hauts de Palayson". Go straight on until the street becomes boulevard Palayson. At number 40 is a discreet notice on the letterbox: "Musée Varois du Scoutisme".

A modest, not to say secretive, place, not found in guidebooks and unknown at the local tourist office, the Musée Varois du Scoutisme nevertheless throws some interesting light on the history and universality of the Scout movement.

> **When abbé Pierre was known as "Contemplative Beaver" …**

Started by père Laurent Eplé, the museum is installed in a cellar of his house, which by the way offers a superb view of the rock of Roquebrune-sur-Argens (see below)

Apart from the insignia of the various scouting movements and the special merit badges which will particularly interest fans of the movement and former scouts, the museum lets you follow the evolution of scouting over several decades. You can see how the clothing has been adapted (the word "uniform" isn't used) with, for example, since 1941 the adoption of a beret to replace the Baden Powell "cowboy" hat.

Beside the patrol pennants are exhibited the "good scout" totems, batons bearing personalized symbols recalling that everyone was named after an animal together with a descriptive adjective. Abbé Pierre* was thus known as "Contemplative Beaver", Simone Veil as "Agitated Hare", François Léotard as "Idealistic Zebra", Michel Rocard as "Learned Hamster" and Jacques Martin as "Optimistic Frog".

You may like to know that collectors of scouting ephemera meet every year in Leven, Belgium, on the last weekend of October. Some of them specialize in adverts featuring scouts (*Vache qui rit* cheese, Wonder torch batteries, etc.), while others collect stamps with scouting images …

*Abbé Pierre, a Roman Catholic priest, was France's leading champion of the destitute and homeless, founding the Emmaus hostel movement in 1953 . He died in January 2007 aged 94.

## SCOUTING

Founded in 1907 by Baden Powell, scouting is a movement aimed at developing a sense of responsibility and respect for traditional values among children and young people. La Fédération du Scoutisme Français has around 80,000 members, bringing together the Éclaireuses et Éclaireurs de France (secular), the Éclaireuses et Éclaireurs unionistes de France (Protestant, set up in 1911), the Éclaireurs israélites de France (Jewish), the Scouts et Guides de France (Catholic) and the Scouts musulmans de France (Muslim).

## THE CHAPEL DOOR AT CHÂTEAU DU ROUËT

CD47, 83490 Le Muy
• Open Monday to Saturday, 8.30–12.00 and 14.00–18.00 (19.00 in summer)
• Sundays and public holidays 14.00–18.00
• Tel. 04 94 99 21 10 • E-mail: info@rouet.com • www.chateau-du-rouet.com
• Chapel visits by arrangement

*A curious relic of the Napoleonic era*

The chapel of the château du Rouët has some rather distinctive fixtures, such as the cabin door of the *Belle Poule*, a frigate that left Toulon to bring the ashes of the emperor Napoleon Bonaparte to Paris. (For details of the *Belle Poule*'s arrival at Courbevoie, see *Banlieue de Paris insolite et secrète* in this series of guidebooks).

The Rouët domain dates back to 1927, the year of the fire that ravaged the region from Les Arcs to Mandelieu. Having bought the land, the ancestors of the present owner, Bernard Savatier, came across a clause in the deeds to which they hadn't paid much attention. They had committed themselves to celebrate a daily mass for the repose of the soul of the respectable sir Verion d'Esclans and his family. So they had to add a chapel to the property, employ a chaplain and provide him with board and lodging on site.

Lucien Savatier, who bought the place, was a naval electrical engineer (he had installed the electricity in the turrets of battleships and the early tanks) and thus was asked to dismantle the *Belle Poule*. He made sure of recuperating the door of the cabin that had housed the imperial ashes and decided to fit out the chapel with it.

---

### SIGHTS NEARBY

#### THE FAULTS OF ROQUEBRUNE: IN MEMORY OF CHRIST' DEATH?

Opposite the scouting museum is a majestic red rock that you can't miss when driving along the A8. On the summit are three crosses that you can just make out from that distance, for which the rock is named: "Rocher des trois croix". It's impossible to get near them because the land is private, shared among 70 properties. Legend has it that the rock split into three sections at the precise moment when Christ died on the Mount of Olives.

Three fractures corresponding to the three crosses of Calvary and the three parts of the Holy Trinity …

The three crosses on the summit of Roquebrune, altitude 373 m, were unveiled on 11 July 1991. The work of sculptor Bernard Venet who divides his time between New York and Le Muy, they each weigh over a tonne and are 4.75 m high. They pay tribute to three of the great painters in the history of art: Giotto, who decorated the Scrovegni chapel in Padua, Italy, in the 14th century, Grünewald and El Greco. Bernard Venet was inspired by these three artists and their representations of the crucifixion.

## EAT AT THE FERME DU RABINON ❿

RD25, 83490 Le Muy
• Tel. 04 94 45 18 53
• Access: After leaving the motorway head for Le Muy. At the roundabout before the village, take the first exit on the right. Following the RD25, cross the River Argens and drive past the kayak centre. The farm is just after that on the left.

> *An unusual and convivial meal*

Renaud Vassas is an extraordinary character. To say that his farm meals are unusual is an understatement, taking account of the surreal experience of this strange environment where car bodies jostle for space with indefinable objects and works of art made from soldered iron.

A versatile artist, Renaud also "exhibits" abroad (Moscow, Stockholm): he simply fills up his truck, unloads them and sells the lot …

At home, he divides his time between recuperation of found objects, the raw materials of his art, and his vocation of host to large convivial sessions around the table. These run along the following lines: everyone sits at the same table where skillets are set out for cooking generous servings of *foie gras*. Beforehand you may help yourself to *rillettes de canard* [potted duck], finely sliced duck breast [*magret*], rissole potatoes, and you can finish up with salads and home-made sorbets. But don't forget to bring along your own wine because it's not included in the €34 menu and not supplied by the house. The meal is above all a chance to put the world to rights with merry strangers, to laugh and drink a toast, even if you have forgotten to bring a bottle, because your dining companions, regular visitors, won't let you die of thirst …

Photo of the host and artist Renaud Vassas

# THE AERIAL WELL AT TRANS

Chemin de la Côte
83720 Trans-en-Provence

*Water
from air*

**A**n extraordinary creation of Belgian engineer Achille Knapen, the *puits aérien* [aerial well] at Trans-en-Provence was aimed at no less than resolving the problem of drought in Africa. The idea was to recuperate water from condensation (steam on windows and dew on plants) in an immense tower built especially for the purpose.

Inspired by the ruins of Feodosiya in the Crimea (Ukraine), he decided to test his idea with a full-size model. Trans was chosen for its hot climate, which he (wrongly) thought resembled North African conditions. In 1931 this aerial well of impressive dimensions – 12 m in diameter, 12 m high and walls 2.5 m thick – was inaugurated.

Briefly, it works like this: warm air circulates inside the tower during the day and, at night, the cold air coming into contact with the remains of the warm air condenses into water vapour. This, collected inside the well, then runs into an underground reservoir.

The results were disappointing. Achille Knapen only collected the equivalent of a bucketful per night: well bellow expectations for the project. There was no follow-up. Perhaps a missed opportunity, however, bearing in mind that the variations in temperature in summer in this part of Provence are very much less than those of the desert regions of North Africa, with a more "continental" type climat …

## SIGHTS NEARBY

### AUBERGE DU VIEUX MOULIN

Place des Moulins
83720 Trans-en-Provence
• Tel. 04 94 70 87 59
• E-mail: contact@auberge-la-grotte.com
• www.auberge-la-grotte.com
• Menus at €18, €28, €38 and €45
• Dinner dances, banquets, weddings

Established as its name indicates in a former mill, the restaurant du Vieux Moulin has a particularly impressive dining room, set up in St Catherine's cave. The cave used to be a place of pilgrimage for the region's millers, who came each 25 November to beg their patron saint for a good harvest.

# MUSÉE DE L'ARTILLERIE

Avenue de la Grande-Armée
Quartier Bonaparte  83300 Draguignan
• Tel. 04 98 10 83 85 et 86
• E-mail: musee.artillerie@worldonline.fr
• Open Sunday to Wednesday 9.00–12.00 and 13.30–17.30
• Admission free

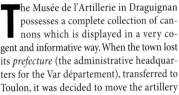

The Musée de l'Artillerie in Draguignan possesses a complete collection of cannons which is displayed in a very cogent and informative way. When the town lost its *prefecture* (the administrative headquarters for the Var département), transferred to Toulon, it was decided to move the artillery school of Châlons-en-Champagne to Draguignan by way of compensation. A few years later, in 1976, the museum was naturally set up there too.

*A remarkable gas mask for a horse*

A visit lets you understand history from the point of view of the artillery, constantly present in any military or civil conflicts that France was involved in.

Thus you learn that the seal with which the cannons were stamped (Louis XIV, Napoleon, RF for République Française or LP for Louis-Philippe) didn't stop them from firing on the workers who cast them … Among the museum's treasures are a few cannons bearing inscriptions for the benefit of the gunners, like the handle you have to turn a certain way to raise the barrel, under which you can read the simple instruction "*plus loin*" [a bit further]. The defensive artefacts include some of the most unusual pieces, such as this remarkable horse's gas mask. Until the second half of the 20th century, the only way of moving a cannon was with the aid of a horse to pull it. So a mask was invented suitable for the gunner's best friend … In the same vein, don't miss the baby's gas mask, so large that you have the impression of looking at a baby in a jar.

ANNVS
MDCCXXXII.
XXII. Omnipotenti
IRATO, ET ANGELO EIVS
VINDICI, CONTAGIOSA
LVE POPVLVM HVIVS
PROVIC. PERCVTIENTI,
INTERCESSIONE DEIPARÆ
ETFICACITER OPPOSVERVNT
CIVES DRAGVENSES

NOBILES CONSVLATV
FRANCISCO NOE DE RASCAS, 1743

720-21-22  Au Tout-Puissant irrité et à son ange vengeur
ppant de la contagion de la PESTE le Peuple de cette provi
abitants de DRAGUIGNAN ont opposé efficacement l'intercession de la Mère de

# CHAPELLE NOTRE-DAME-DU-PEUPLE

Rue Notre-Dame-du-Peuple
83700 Draguignan

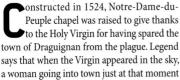

*A picture
that lost
its head ...*

Constructed in 1524, Notre-Dame-du-Peuple chapel was raised to give thanks to the Holy Virgin for having spared the town of Draguignan from the plague. Legend says that when the Virgin appeared in the sky, a woman going into town just at that moment with a bundle of washing felt her load grow so heavy, she could no longer carry it ... Alerted by the citizens, the town consuls came to examine the bundle and understood that it had been contaminated by the plague. Anti-plague measures taken early enough meant that Draguignan avoided the terrible disease.

The chapel stood on the Royal Road that used to link the town to Lorgues and Aix-en-Provence. In the 18th century it was decided to build a wider road that no longer passed before the chapel, which found itself off the beaten track again.

Inside the chapel are many marble ex-votos but hardly any painted ones: 70 of them were stolen in 1974 and the remaining few are now in Draguignan's Musée des Arts et Traditions Populaires.

Two works are of particular note: the Rosary Virgin, painting on wood from the Bréa school, and a picture whose history adds to its interest. Painted by père Valentin de l'Observance, it shows a procession with a Latin caption underneath that reads: "1720–21–22. To the Almighty and his avenging angel striking down with the contagion of the plague the people of this province, the inhabitants of Draguignan expeditiously opposed the intervention of the Mother of God. Under the consulship of Noble Joseph de Rasque, Seigneur de Taradeau ...". Looking closely at the picture, pay special attention to Joseph de Rasque, the main figure on the left. A local nobleman, his head was cut out of the canvas during the Revolution and later replaced by another ... You can see this "cover-up", which says a lot for the state of mind of the 1789 revolutionaries, with the naked eye. The picture is a reminder that once more Draguignan had been spared the plague that ravaged Provence from 1720.

## ÉCOLE DES BRÉA

The Bréa school was founded by Louis Bréa, an artist from Nice born around 1450 and who died in 1523. His numerous works on religious themes (frescoes, retables, triptychs) which can be found from Nice to Genoa as well as in the outlying towns and villages, marked the break with Gothic art and the irruption of the Renaissance. The name of the movement is plural because several members of his family, such as François Bréa, followed the same vocation.

## THE FAIRY STONE

Route de Montferrat 83300 Draguignan
• 1 km from town centre
• The dolmen is on private property but not enclosed

### *The largest dolmen on the Côte d'Azur*

Even if you've already seen plenty of dolmens, the massive size of the "Fairy Stone", serenely standing in a beautiful green setting, is always something of a shock. With its horizontal slab estimated at some 25 tonnes, the entire Fairy Stone, 6 m long and 2.35 m high, weighs around 60 tonnes. It is thought to have been erected 2,500 years ago and served as a sacrificial altar for Druidic ceremonies.

The name of the stone has its roots in legend: a fairy disguised as a shepherdess had asked her sweetheart to make her a bed from a heavy stone supported by two others. After exhausting efforts to assemble the three stones and set two of them upright, there was no way that the suitor could lift or put in place the stone that was to serve as a bed. So the fairy raised the stone using her supernatural powers, to the surprise of the young man. Of true Mediterranean temperament, he couldn't bear the insult and slunk away to die.

Frédéric Mistral mentions the stone in his poem *Calendal* in which the heroine, last princess of Les Baux, is called Esterelle.

You also may be surprised by the upper part of one of the supporting stones which has obviously been restored (and by the way covered in graffiti). The damage was done by some Draguignan residents dynamiting the stone because they didn't accept the transfer, in 1974, of Var Préfecture from their town to Toulon. So they took their revenge on the symbol that proved that their town had precedence over the Mediterranean port of war.

N.B.: *dolmen* comes from the Breton word for "stone table".

---

### SIGHTS NEARBY

#### INSCRIPTION ON THE WALL OF RAYOL VIADUCT
Viaduc du Rayol. Former railway line 83830 Claviers
• Access: following the RD55 in the direction of Grasse, 5.5 km from the village, take the road to the left signposted "voie ferrée". Carry on along this narrow track, going under two bridges until you reach the viaduct projecting over the Rayol valley.

On the impressive Rayol viaduct, at the end of the bridge on the right, you can read the curious inscription "*Mort à Guillaume*" on a low wall. Carved by conscripts of the canton of Fayence leaving for the front lines during the First World War, along with their initials, the invective was addressed to the Kaiser, William II, last German Emperor and last King of Prussia. Although he was not the direct cause of the outbreak of war, the Kaiser had prepared for it with intense rearmament and did nothing to avoid it. The only thing he represented to these conscripts was a monarch of an enemy country, from whom Alsace and Lorraine had to be retaken since the French defeat of 1870.

# MUSÉE DES MINÉRAUX ET FOSSILES

19, rue François-Maurel 83830 Bargemon
• For opening hours, which are subject to change, enquire at **Bargemon tourist office**: 1, avenue Pasteur 83830 Bargemon
• Tel: 04 94 47 81 73 • Admission: €2

*Mystery of the uncoiling ammonites*

**B**argemon's Musée des Minéraux et Fossiles, owned by the village *mairie*, offers over 3,000 examples. Although the minerals come from all over the world, most of the fossils were discovered locally. There are many ammonites on display, included some astonishing uncoiled specimens.

The Alpes-Maritimes region, but above all, neighbouring Alpes-de-Haute-Provence, has the greatest number and the finest specimens of uncoiled ammonites. A period of geological time even bears the name Barremian stage in reference to the village of Barrême (Alpes-de-Haute-Provence), a typical site.

**AMMONITES**

An ammonite, or ammonoid, is an extinct marine cephalopod mollusc, coiled like a snail shell, which owes its name to Amon's horn, a spiral-shaped ram's horn that adorned the head of the Egyptian deity Amon. Ammonites appeared in the Devonian (Paleozoic era, around 400 million years ago) and disappeared at the end of the Cretaceous (Mesozoic era, around 100 million years ago).

The hypothesis of a meteorite impact in the Gulf of Mexico (which caused the circular shape of the gulf) towards the end of the Cretaceous period and the beginning of the Tertiary era (called the KT limit by scientists) is accepted by the majority of the scientific community today. There is no longer much doubt that this impact would have plunged the Earth into darkness by the mass of material flung into the atmosphere and would have caused the extinction of the dinosaurs (and that of the ammonites).

## EX-VOTO FOR AN ELECTRICAL STORM

Notre-Dame-de-l'Ormeau 83440 Seillans
• Guided tours every Thursday at 11.00, also Tuesday at 17.30 in July and
August • Contribution: €2 • Booking at Seillans tourist office

*Dry and*
*silent lightning*

It's difficult to define the climatic phenomenon that struck Seillans in April 1892.
Some call it a "magnetic storm", others an
"electrical storm", but many of the inhabitants blamed the electricity "fairy"
for being behind it.

At the beginning of the year 1892, Viscountess Savigny de Moncorps obtained permission from the authorities to be connected to the electricity sup-
ply to power her perfumery. There was one condition: the houses on the road
leading to the perfumery were also to be connected. A short time afterwards,
in April 1892, there arrived a particular storm with flashes of lightning but no
thunder or rain. A dry and silent storm, in a way, which terrorized the population. These flashes even penetrated the houses without causing any injuries
or damage. Clearly, it was the new-fangled electrical energy that was to blame
for having offended God, the sole keeper of invisible forces. But as the phenomenon seemed to have only been a warning, with no further consequences, the
residents thanked the Virgin and the Good Lord. An ex-voto showing a lightning fork entering a house was painted and put on display in the Notre-
Dame-de-l'Ormeau chapel and a cross bearing an inscription that reads "In
memory of the electrical storm" was erected beside Saint-Cyr chapel. For some
unknown reason, the cross disappeared and part of it was later found at the
Seillans dump by the organizers of the Musée du Souvenir – 15 août 1944,
where it has been on display ever since.

MUSÉE DU SOUVENIR - 15 AOÛT 1944
ZA La Bégude 83440 Brovès-en-Seillans
• Open daily 14.00–18.00 • Guided tours: adults €4, children €2 • Tel. 04 94 84 77 93

**SIGHTS NEARBY**

### THE TWO ROCKS OF SEILLANS
Place Font-d'Amont 83440 Seillans

Just beside the Saracen gate, two rocky outcrops emerge oddly from the
ground on a level with the nearby houses. In the 1950s, the houses built on
them collapsed for no apparent reason. It so happened that the local residents had all gone to a funeral that day, while the children were taking advantage of the one day in the week when there was no school, at that time,
to watch the only television in the village. Miraculously, nobody was hurt in
the incident.

The two rocks have been classed as historic monuments and you can imagine how narrow the rooms must be in the houses round about. In fact they
had been built on the former ramparts.

# THE VILLAGE OF BROVÈS

Brovès-en-Seillans
83440 Seillans

*The village
that moved
house*

I f individuals move regularly enough and if sometimes certain buildings are transported stone by stone to a different site, it is rare for entire villages to "move house". Yet that's what happened to Brovès-en-Seillans, which now stands at the junction of the RD562 and the RD53 in the commune of Seillans. Its original site, on the RD25 north of Bargemon, was within the catchment area of the military camp at Canjuers.

Between 1969 and 1972, the plateau of Canjuers was taken over by the army and turned into a war games training area of 35,000 hectares. Today there are 5,000–6,000 personnel at this camp, but the "militarization" of this zone was not without repercussions: the fight against the expansion of Larzac camp being well covered at the time by the media, the affair of Canjuers, despite the low population density, was quickly taken up too. In vain: on 4 August 1970, the village of Brovès was "moved" 35 km from its original site and renamed Brovès-en-Seillans.

From the road, old village of Brovès is a poignant sight: the church has kept its bell tower (but not its bell) and the slate roofs, most of them collapsed, have been replaced by brick red tiles. It is strictly prohibited to enter the village and, other than the sanctions risked by those who disobey, the state of the buildings poses a serious risk to anyone venturing into the streets.

On the other hand, the new hamlet of Brovès-en-Seillans looks like a housing estate. The only things remaining from the original village are the fountain and the war memorial. Without forgetting that the gravestones were also moved from the old cemetery.

SEILLANS TOURIST OFFICE
1, rue du Valat 83440 Seillans
• Tel: 04 94 76 85 91• Fax: 04 94 39 13 53

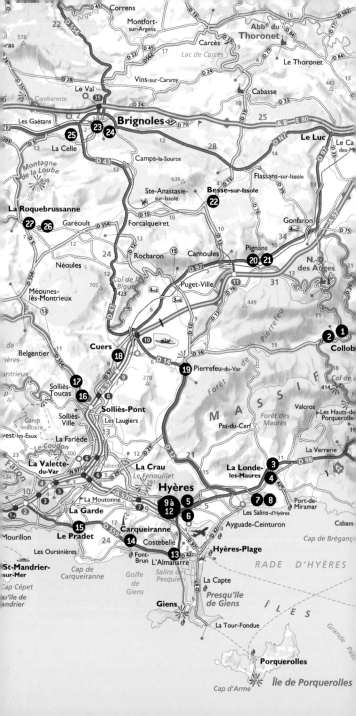

# IN AND AROUND HYÈRES

# THE LAMBERT MENHIRS

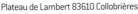

Plateau de Lambert 83610 Collobrières

• Access by foot only from Collobrières: either by the GR90 from the village (75 minutes walk down a steep slope), or else by the forest road that starts at the Anselme cross, also a 1 hr. 15 min. walk. To take this more level route, leave Collobrières in the direction of Grimaud. At the fork 3 km from the village, turn the right towards Grimaud. 2.8 km further, take the right turn towards the Chartreuse de la Verne. About 200 m onwards, to the right, you will find a parking area where you may leave your car. The forest road, strictly prohibited to vehicles, starts just behind the car park. The menhirs stand on the Lambert plateau 6 km further on, just after the forest house.

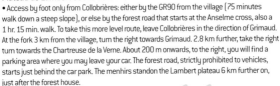

**The mystery remains**

O n the magnificent Lambert plateau, 471 m in altitude, are two of the most beautiful menhirs (3.15 and 2.82 metres tall) to be found in Var, and without a doubt, in the entire south-east of France. Dating from a period somewhere between the end of the Neolithic Period and the end of the Bronze Age, these two monoliths consist of micaceous gneiss from the local area, and it is believed that they were extracted from a site located only a hundred metres from where they now stand. What was the purpose of these two menhirs? Markers, primitive idols, energy reservoirs? The mystery remains.

Around the menhirs, you can admire some very beautiful hundred-year-old chestnut trees as well as some colossal tree stumps.

## SIGHTS NEARBY

### MAIRIE DE COLLOBRIÈRES

Place de la Libération-15-Août-1944 83610 Collobrières

• Open 9.00–12.00 and 15.30–17.30 Monday to Friday

In the entry hall of Collobrières town hall, two glass display cases present minerals from the massif des Maures, including some very curious garnets incrusted in mica schist. These garnets are opaque and lack the transparency needed to obtain precious stones, compared with garnets from Bohemia.

### THE BIGGEST DOLMEN IN VAR : THE GAOUTABRY DOLMEN

Piste Notre-Dame-des-Maures 83250 La Londe-les-Maures

• Access: the trail, practicable but closed to ordinary traffic, starts from the RD88, 4 km north of the village. A signpost indicates the way to the dolmen. Allow about 45 minutes to walk there, on this wide path with a gentle slope.

Discovered in 1876, the Gaoutabry* dolmen, dating from the end of the Neolithic and the beginning of the use of copper (2500 BC), is one of the oldest dolmens in the region and one of the oldest vestiges discovered within this commune, testifying to a human presence going back to the Chalcolithic Age. Listed as a historic monument since 1988, the dolmen is rectangular, covering a surface area of 9 m². Constructed using slabs of phyllite, cut out of rocks in the surrounding area and assembled on site, this dolmen, like most others in Provence, lacks horizontal 'table' slab on top. Such a slab may perhaps have been broken up at some point and the debris dispersed, or else the dolmen had a roof composed of plant material resting on logs, as suggested by the slots found on the lateral slabs and the interstices between them.

* Derived from the Provençal words *caud* (warm) and *gaouto* (ridge of a hill) as well as the French word *abri* (shelter), the name of this funeral shelter thus evokes its position on top of a warm, sunlit hill.

# LA CHEMINÉE-TUNNEL DE LA LONDE    ❹

La Fonderie 83250 La Londe-les-Maures
• Access: To see the chimney-tunnel in its entirety, but from a distance, the best spot is the Ducourneau roundabout (car park). To approach the chimney itself, better abandon any idea of going by car. By way of promenade des Annamites and chemin d'Azureva (on foot), you can bypass the vacation village on the left and then see the start of the tunnel, protected by a high fence. The best solution, however, is to sign up for the guided tour regularly organized by the tourist office at La Londe, called "Sur les traces des mineurs" [On the miners' trail].
• Admission: €3.50.

## *The longest chimney in Europe*

The discovery of rich veins of lead and zinc around 1875 was the starting-point of a veritable economic boom in the neighbourhood of La Londe. The village was then able to demand its administrative separation from the Hyères commune, which it obtained in 1901.

With an annual output of about 7 million tonnes of ore, the mines of La Londe were one of the most important metal-producing mines in France. A railway provided transport for the workforce and took the ore from various deposits to the port of L'Argentière. You can follow the now-vanished railway track by walking along chemin des Annamites.

This mine of course had an enormous impact on the landscape, which is still marked by various buildings and other vestiges of mining activity: shafts, galleries, slanted tunnels for raising and descending material, stands for machinery, ramps, washing basins, a smeltery, miners' cottages, and administra-

tive offices. But the most remarkable element in this rich mining heritage is the chimney-tunnel for the lead smeltery, built in 1897 on an experimental basis along more than a kilometre of hillside, making it the longest of its kind in Europe.

The exhaustion of the Argentière vein and the fall in mineral prices from 1904 onwards led to a gradual abandonment of the mine, which finally ceased operations altogether in 1929. At that point, the Schneider company opened a torpedo factory in La Londe.

OFFICE DE TOURISME DE LA LONDE-LES-MAURES
Avenue Albert-Roux 83250 La Londe-les-Maures
• Tel: 04 94 01 53 10 • Fax : 04 94 01 53 19
• E-mail: lalonde.tourisme@wanadoo.fr • www.ot-lalondelesmaures.fr

# PARC SAINTE-CLAIRE

Avenue Edith-Warthon
83400 Hyères
• Open November to March, 8.00–17.00; April, May, September, and October, 8.00–18.00; and June to August, 8.00–19.00.
• Admission free

> *The chateau of the man who discovered the Venus de Milo*

**F**rom the Sainte-Claire park overlooking the town of Hyères, the view of the Îles d'Or, the Giens peninsula and the inland countryside is superb. The offices of the Parc National de Port-Cros (and the Conservatoire Botanique National de Porquerolles) are housed in a curious Baroque chateau that looks like it is made out of cardboard.

Olivier Voutier, its first owner, is buried within the park, in the Drapeau tower above the chateau. A naval officer born in Thouars (Deux-Sèvres), Voutiers sailed from Toulon aboard the schooner *L'Estafette*, which stopped at Melos (Milo), an island in the Cyclades archipelago of Greece. On 8 April 1820, this archaeology enthusiast met a peasant named Yorgos who had unearthed a marble statue. The Venus de Milo had come to light. Voutier was determined to bring this masterpiece back to France, but lacked the financial and diplomatic means (Greece was still a Turkish dependency). The French Government dispatched the famous explorer Dumont-Durville to conclude the deal and four months later the statue arrived at the Louvre. In 1821, Olivier Voutier resigned from the French royal navy due to his aversion to the Restoration monarchy and enlisted out of conviction with the Greek army fighting for independence. He was given the rank of colonel and upon retirement, settled down in Hyères. There he had the Castel Sainte-Claire built on the model of the fort of Talente, opposite Negropont (a Greek island, now called Euboea, off the coast of Boeotia), where he had fought. It is said that his last dying word was: "Venus".

## SIGHTS NEARBY

### A STONE USED TO PREDICT THE FUTURE

You can also enter the park from rue Saint-Claire. Turning right at the park entrance, walk up rue Saint-Pierre and a little further on you will come across an unusual stone marked with numerous small hollows, or "cupules". This cupule stone, 13 m long and 3 m wide, dates back to the Neolithic Period. It is believed that it was used to predict the future by observing the path taken by water running through the maze of these cupules, hollowed out by hand with primitive tools.

### THE SALT ROAD

For nearly six centuries, the Salt Road meant fortune or ruin for the staging-posts along the way. Thousands of mules, each carrying almost 80 kilos of load, or *"charge"* (an actual standard unit of weight in the County of Nice), travelled on difficult trails through the snowy passes of the Alps.

The itinerary took into account both natural obstacles and political factors. The valley of the Var River, for example, which formed the border with the Provençal states, was considered too exposed, while the valleys of the Tinée (in the hands of the Grimaldi) and the Roia (held by the Lascaris de Tende) failed to offer sufficient guarantees of safe passage due to their unstable sovereignties.

The convoys left by way of the valley of the Paillon River (which flows into Nice) and halted to refresh themselves at Saint-André-de-la-Roche. A first version of the route ran through L'Escarène, Lucéram, and Sospel by making a long detour to avoid the gorges of the Vésubie river. But in 1433, a new route was pioneered by an extraordinary figure: Paganino del Pozzo, an *entrepreneur de gabelle* (*) from Nice whose family had settled at Cuneo. He proposed to build a faster and safer road at his own expense, in exchange for a toll on the goods that would be transported upon it. His route passed through Levens and Utelle, where loads were weighed to make sure they matched the amounts declared. In all, it took about a day and a half to reach Saint-Martin-Vésubie, the last stop before the Alpine passes, whose prosperity was based on its status as a storehouse for goods in transit between Piedmont and the Mediterranean. Depending on circumstances, a convoy would cross the Alps by the pass at Madone de Fenestre (see Saint-Martin-Vésubie page 99) or by the Arnovo pass. It would then enter Italy by way of Borgo-San-Dalmazzo and Cuneo.

Paganino, whose name people quickly corrupted "Pagari" (*pagare* meaning "to pay" in Italian), built a sumptuous house, called "Paganino" or the "Salt Palace", still visible today on Via Roma in Cuneo. But he ruined himself in later life by trying to extend his concept of the Salt Road to the Roia valley. He is nevertheless remembered in a saying that sums up better than any long speech the fatalism of the local people: *"Tant que Pagari paghara Lo Pas passara; Quant Pagari paghara plus Lo pas passara plus..."* (roughly translatable as "As long as Pagari [Paganino del Pozzo] pays, the pass will remain open"). However, there is also a variant that adds a perfidious reflexive Italian "si", giving: "As long as Pagari GETS paid (i.e. collects his toll), the pass will remain open."

(*) The *entrepreneurs de gabelle* or *gabeliers* were individuals to whom the Dukes of Savoy conceded rights over salt transport and the collection of salt taxes.

To find out more: *La Route du sel* [The Salt Road], Henry Mouton, collection L'Ancre Solaire, Éditions Serre, Nice.

# VIEUX-SALINS D'HYÈRES

Port Pothuau
Les Salins-d'Hyères
83400 Hyères

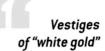

*Vestiges of "white gold"*

**M**ontmajour abbey, near Arles, began to dry out the swamps east of Hyères in order to convert them into salt marshes. The technique changed little in subsequent periods: the basic idea was to draw seawater, each litre of which contains about 30 grammes of sodium chloride (the scientific name for ordinary salt), into evaporation basins known as "*tables*". After that, all one needed to do was to wait for crystallization to occur before harvesting the natural product.

If salt was "the noblest of foods, the condiment par excellence" according to Plutarch, it was also used as a major preserving agent in the past. Relatively scarce, salt was therefore expensive, and those in power have always taxed it heavily (see the definition of the *gabelle*, or salt tax, on page 173, in connection with the salt chair of Gourdon).

Other than its use by local inhabitants, the salt from Salins-d'Hyères was at the origin of the legendary "Salt Road" leading to the Piedmont region from the 14th to 19th centuries: the salt was transported first by barge or *felucca*, unloaded at Nice, and then taken in convoy overland on the backs of donkeys or mules. In Nice, the salt from Salins-d'Hyères was stored in lofts at cours Saleya (hence its name).

The *treuil* at Salins-d'Hyères, a sort of emergency sluice-gate, is found on the bridge crossing the little canal that runs into the sea. It served to close the gate of the covered canal where vessels loaded with their precious cargo waited for daylight to set sail. This dissuaded thieves and *faux-sauniers* (salt smugglers) attracted by the presence of "white gold".

It should be noted that Salins-des-Pesquiers, located on the Giens peninsula, was created artificially in 1848. This site, along with that of Salins-d'Hyères, ceased activity not very long ago (Hyères in 1966 and Pesquiers in 2001). The Conservatoire du Littoral, the agency responsible for protecting the French coasts, has now acquired ownership of all the salt marshes.

# LA RÉSIDENCE SIMONE BERRIAU

**❽**

22-28, boulevard du Front-de-Mer
Les Salins-d'Hyères
83400 Hyères
- Three-room luxury apartment for seasonal lettings.
- Panoramic view, air-conditioning.
- From €350 to €800 per week depending on the season.
- Contact (Tel) Anne-Lise Mortelmans at 04 94 38 94 72 or at 06 84 39 83 42 (mobile) • E-mail: annelisemortelmans@hotmail.com

*Celebrity
residence*

I f flats with a view of the sea and the islands, a private sandy beach (only 10 m from the building), a swimming pool, and private boat dock are relatively common, the Simone Berriau residence offers something more.

Seeing her artistic career as an opera singer was blocked by a persistent grain of pepper lodged in her vocal cords (!), Simone Berriau got involved at the beginning of 1940s in theatre production. Owner of the Antoine theatre, she frequented artistic circles and one day decided that she would very much like to gather all these beautiful people together for a holiday in the south of France. The idea thus grew of a residence where all the co-owners would be from show business. In 1963, the three buildings were ready and people such as Marcel Achard, Jean Richard, Georges Guétary, Robert Dhéry, André Castelot, Michel Serrault, Jacques Legras, Louisde Funès, along with many other stars of the stage or cinema, started to be seen there.

Baptized "Cat on a Hot Tin Roof", "View from the Bridge", and "The Dazzling Hour" the apartments are all part of a residence conceived by the Toulon architect, Pierre Pascalet. He also designed some immense mosaics and the external walkways connected by stairwells in the form of round towers. Today, more than 40 years after it was built, the Simone Berriau has not gone out of fashion and proudly bears its architectural style, very similar to that of the Hôtel Latitude 43 constructed by the architect Pingusson in Saint-Tropez (and at present standing empty).

Although many of the artists have disappeared and their apartments resold to more anonymous residents, people in Hyères still revere the name of Simone Berriau. In the early 1970s, it was she who persuaded the French Prime Minister, Pierre Messmer, to order the pilots at the naval airbase in Hyères to interrupt their training during the month of August ...

# ALL SAINTS CHURCH

Boulevard Félix-Descroix
83400 Hyères

*An abandoned Anglican chapel*

Hidden away in a copse of pine trees, All Saints Church is located opposite Gustave-Roux middle school in the Costebelle neighbourhood. It can only be seen from the outside, the land on which it sits having been fenced off to discourage squatters. Left abandoned, it is now in a poor state of repair and nothing has been done about preserving it, despite its historical interest. In the 19th century, Hyères had become a favorite winter haunt for the English, and Queen Victoria herself, who stayed in the south of France on several occasions, visited Hyères in 1892. Although there had been a place of worship in the town since 1852 and an Anglican church built in a neogothic style was consecrated in 1884 (see below), the queen wanted to have a chapel close to the hotels in Costebelle where she resided, so that she could go there several times each day. So she had All Saints Church built in 1892. But the queen never returned to Hyères and the chapel gradually fell into disuse.

## SIGHTS NEARBY

### ÉGLISE ANGLICANE
22, avenue David-Beauregard
(corner of avenue Godillot)
83400 Hyères

The Anglican church at Hyères was built by the architect Chapoulart in 1883-1884 on land provided by the property developer and industrialist Alexis Godillot (whose name also entered French military history as the designer of French soldiers' boots). Although Anglican services were held here until 1950, the church has today become a municipal cultural centre. In the garden surrounding the church, a particularly anachronistic road sign has been preserved, reading: "Avenue Alexis-Godillot. Vehicles lacking suspension forbidden passage." This was meant to prevent carts and other types of carriage from damaging the avenue's fragile bitumen surface.

### CHAPELLE NOTRE-DAME-DE-CONSOLATION
Boulevard Félix-Descroix 83400 Hyères

Close by the Pomponiana institute (voir page 229), and just above All Saints Church, another Virgin with Child, equally monumental, seems to be standing crooked on the façade of the Notre-Dame-de-Consolation church. The coloured cement statue was made by Jean-Lambert Rucki, an artist born in Poland who shared Modigliani's bohemian life.

# LA FONTAINE MARIANNE STEWART  ⑫

Place Théodore-Lefebvre 83400 Hyères

> *"Be good to animals, never forget that they work for us and suffer like us."*

The fountain that stands in place Théodore-Lefebvre in Hyères, in front of the media library, is in fact a drinking trough for animals. It was commissioned by a British resident, and built after her death, in thanks to the town of Hyères for having made her welcome and to quench the thirst of its four-legged inhabitants.

"The Metropolitan Drinking Fountain and Cattle Trough Association", today shortened to "The Drinking Fountain Association", was founded in England in 1859. Queen Victoria was one of the its financial contributors, and like Marianne Stewart in Hyères, she gave money to her hosts on the French Riviera to build watering places that were intended mainly for animals.

In Hyères, the Marianne Stewart drinking trough supplies six basins, two of them with very low rims. But one should point out that most of the time there's nary a cat to be seen in the vicinity of this monument ... As for humans, they

can also refresh the mind by reading the bilingual text carved in Cassis stone: "In affectionate memory of Marianne Stewart deceased on 18 August 1900 after having enjoyed the beauty and climate of Hyères for many years. She dedicated herself to humane works and her last desire was that a drinking trough be built to refresh the animals in the town she loved so much. This bequest was fulfilled by her friend and collaborator G.L. Bagnell." On the opposite side of the trough are these words, whose author remains unknown: "Be good to animals, never forget that they work for us and suffer like us."

To find out more about the humanitarian missions of The Drinking Fountain Association: www.drinkingfountains.org

# L'INSTITUT DE RÉÉDUCATION
## FONCTIONNELLE POMPONIANA OLBIA

**13**

Route de l'Almanarre 83407 Hyères
• Tel: 04 94 35 94 35

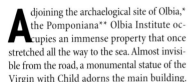

> *A monumental Virgin with Child watches over the patients*

Adjoining the archaelogical site of Olbia,\* the Pomponiana\*\* Olbia Institute occupies an immense property that once stretched all the way to the sea. Almost invisible from the road, a monumental statue of the Virgin with Child adorns the main building. Executed in 1937 by Carlo Sarrabezolles, the 6.5 m high statue was sculpted using a technique invented by the artist: without a scale model and by directly cutting the concrete as it set (the artist was therefore forced to finish his work in a very short time, before the concrete hardened).

The history of this institute is representative of Hyère's medical role in the 19th and early 20th centuries. For patients suffering from consumption, it offered, if not a cure, at least a place to spend their final days in the sunshine, under the palm trees ... Several sanatoriums thus flourished, right by the shore or on the heights above the town, including the Pomponiana, created by the canon Mourot (1866-1948). Opened in 1923, the institute specialized in treating tuberculosis until 1979 and today welcomes patients with cerebromotor handicaps.

To find out more about the sculptor Carlo Sarrabezolles, see the following site: http://sarrabezolles.chez-alice.fr

\* Olbia: a commercial outpost founded in the 4th century BC by Greek sailors who arrived from Massalia. *Olbia* is Greek for "happy".
\*\* Pomponiana: in the 2nd century BC, the Romans established a base for their galleys next to Olbia and named it Pomponiana.

---

**SIGHTS NEARBY**

### LA FAUSSE TOMBE DE SAINT-EXUPÉRY

**14**

Cimetière de Carqueiranne Chemin du Petit-Lac 83320 Carqueiranne
Take the first alley on the left and follow it to the end. The tomb is located against the wall surrounding the cemetery.

At the beginning of the month of September 1944, the body of a pilot was found washed up on the shore of the Port-Maurice cove in Carqueiranne. Pierre Lamazzi, the undertaker at the time, hastened to bury it in a corner of the cemetery. When people became anxious to find out how Antoine de Saint-Exupéry came to disappear and where exactly the wreck of his plane was located, the villagers raised the hypothesis that the body buried in the cemetery, only one month after Saint-Exupéry vanished (31 July 1944), might be that of the author of *The Little Prince*. The grave was thus quickly nicknamed "the writer's tomb" The family having refused any exhumation, the mystery subsisted even after the discovery of the aviator's bracelet offshore from Marseille. It was not until the discovery of the remains of his Lightning P 38, on 24 May 2000 near the island of Riou, that the rumours finally ceased. But to this day, two questions remain unanswered: why did Saint-Exupéry's plane fall into the sea off Marseille, and who is actually buried in the cemetery at Carqueiranne?

# MUSÉE DE LA MINE DU CAP-GARONNE

1000, chemin du Baou-Rouge 83220 Le Pradet
• Tel: 04 94 08 32 46 • Fax: 04 94 08 72 50
• E-mail: info@mine-capgaronne.fr • www.mine-capgaronne.fr
• Opening hours: during French school holidays (all zones), daily 14.00-17.00;
in July and August, 14.00–18.00; outside school holidays, Wednesday,
Saturday, Sunday, and public holidays, 14.00–17.00.
• Admission: adults €6.20; reduced rate €3.80.

> *Unique minerals in an abandoned mine*

Contrary to what its name might suggest, the Cap-Garonne mine is located at Pradet in Var (in Provençal, *garonna* means "stream" or "canal"). The mine has today been turned into an appealing, educational museum and possesses a fabulous underground labyrinth offering a most unusual series of surprises.

Worked during the 19th century to extract copper, the mines were abandoned at the beginning of the 20th century. The subterranean galleries were later transformed into mushroom beds, but from the 1970's onwards, the vogue for minerals began to attract numerous scavengers ... They even went as far as using explosives to uncover the rare minerals and splendid crystals to be found here. A total of 139 minerals have been identified at Cap-Garonne, the most spectacular being azurite, malachite, olivenite and cyanotrichite.

The site is equally unique in the world as the home of 11 new mineralogical species that were described for the first time at Cap-Garonne: capgaronnite, géminite, etc. Several of these rare minerals as well as 600 other specimens are exhibited in the great pyramidal hall, magnificently lit and arranged.

The Cap-Garonne mine is also known to mineralogists across the planet for its micromineralogy collection: various displays give you a glimpse, using optical devices capable of extreme magnifications.

In addition, part of the exhibition shows the various uses of copper. Ranging from naval instruments to copper wire, one appreciates the museum creators' sense of humour in casting copper bells bearing the names of the local government bodies who subsidized the project, the height of each bell being proportional to their respective funding contributions ... The copper heliogravure cylinder, a gift from *Télé 7 jours* magazine, is also surprising, as it prints out TV programmes for the week of 9 July 1994.

## THE TWO CHAPELS OF SAINT CHRISTINE

Chemin de Sainte-Christine, 83210 Solliès-Pont
**Leave the A57 motorway** at Solliès-Pont (exit 7). At the end of the slip road, turn left towards Solliès-Toucas. At the first roundabout turn right, where you'll see a small sign mentioning Sainte-Christine and other directions. After a further 300 m, turn left onto chemin de Sainte-Christine. When you reach the barrier blocking access to vehicles, park your car and expect a 20 minute climb on foot.

### Parochial quarrel

There's a curious sight on the hill overlooking the two villages of Solliès-Toucas and Cuers: the two chapels, both dedicated to St Christine, turn their backs to one another, separated by only a few centimetres across the border between their respective communes.

How did this happen? As the official legend has it, a Greek prince sailing off the shore from Toulon was caught in a storm and swore that if he survived, he would build a chapel to St Christine on the first hill that he glimpsed in the squall. Let us make clear right now that there are two St Christines, one from Tyre who underwent atrocious tortures and always emerged unscathed and smiling, while the other, from Rome, was pierced by arrows near the lake of Bolsena.

The prince survived and the chapel, which was to be built on the hill where the "border" between the two villages passed, provoked a dispute: the two communes could not reach agree, so each built a chapel on its territory, thus illustrating the ordinary foibles of mankind. Even today, the subject is not mentioned in tourist brochures and there are no signs to the chapels.

Both of them are closed more often than not and it is practically impossible to visit them and admire their numerous ex-votos. But the view alone from the top of the hill makes it worth a trip.

| OFFICE DE TOURISME DE CUERS | OFFICE DE TOURISME |
|---|---|
| 18, place de la Convention, 83390 Cuers | DE LA VALLÉE DU GAPEAU |
| • Tel: 04 94 48 56 27 | 5, rue Gabriel-Péri, 83210 Solliès-Pont |
| • Fax: 04 94 28 03 56 | • Tel: 04 94 28 92 35 |
| • E-mail: odt.de.cuers@wanadoo.fr | • Fax: 04 94 33 63 55 |

**SIGHTS NEARBY**

On the marble pediment of the church in the village of Solliès-Toucas is written in gold letters the following curious phrase in Latin: *Sol iste jam ipso bis cruce ligatis aut ecce solis aedes jam veri cruce fulgens* [The sun is already tied twice to the cross; here is the temple of the sun now lit by the true cross]. Above the inscription, a representation of the *sol invictus* makes you daydream of standing before a temple of the sun, waiting for Tintin and the eclipse …

Opposite the church, on the wall of the town hall, is another plaque, not religious in character but still in gold letters on white marble, which commemorates the liberation of the commune from "Germanic hordes" … What a way to prepare for Europe and welcome our neighbours from across the Rhine!

# ST PETER'S ARM

(18)

Notre-Dame de l'Assomption
Place Bernard, 83390 Cuers
• To see St Peter's arm, you'll need to book at the local tourist office.

> *A prestigious religious relic brought from Rome in the 14th century by Gantès the Brave, born at Cuers in 1328*

I n Cuers, St Peter is very present in a most peculiar fashion.

Although the village church is today called Notre-Dame-de-l'Assomption, it was Collégiale Saint-Pierre before the Revolution. Its lateral (and yet main) door is surmounted by a niche in which you can see a statue of St Peter lifting his head.

From the ground, it's difficult to grasp that he's looking at heaven with an angry expression. Nonetheless, it happens to be the case, even if no one can explain why … On the lintel of the door, but here again you'd need to know it was there, you can see the arm of St Peter. This is a stone replica of the extraordinary relic to be found inside the church, in the Saint-Pierre chapel, protected by a wooden door with yet another representation of the saint's arm. The peculiar feature here is that this arm is missing two fingers. If by chance or having booked a visit, this door is opened for you, you'll see behind a tightly meshed iron grill, an arm in vermeil (gilded silver) containing part of the saint's arm.

It was Jean de Gantès ("Gantès the Brave"), born in Cuers in 1328, who brought back from Rome this gift of Pope Clement VI in thanks for his courage and his loyalty to Queen Jeanne of Naples, Countess of Provence.

---

**NICKNAMES GIVEN TO CUERS VILLAGERS**

The *manja sauma* means *"eaters of she-asses"*. This nickname comes from the siege of the village in 1383 by an army from Toulon that obliged the inhabitants to eat she-asses in order to survive. It is also said that it was during the bloody repression of the villagers in Cuers by the soldiers of Louis Napoléon Bonaparte that a blacksmith was forced to eat his apron made from the hide of a she-ass.

The *brulo frema* means the "women burners". This nickname recalls the fact that in 1779 a woman was burned at the stake in Cuers, the last woman accused of witchcraft to suffer this fate in Provence.

# THE DIXMUDE MONUMENT

Boulevard Henri Guérin, 83390 Pierrefeu-du-Var
• Les Amis du Dixmude - Maison des Associations, 83390 Pierrefeu-du-Var
• Contact: Monsieur Tissier (Tel: 04 94 28 23 27)
• Link for a history of dirigibles in Cuers and Pierrefeu-du-Var:
http://perso.wanadoo.fr/m.coterot/

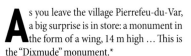

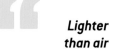

*Lighter than air*

As you leave the village Pierrefeu-du-Var, a big surprise is in store: a monument in the form of a wing, 14 m high … This is the "Dixmude" monument.*

During the First World War, which inaugurated aerial warfare, dirigible balloons demonstrated their efficacy for bombardments, naval or terrestrial reconnaissance, and escorting ship convoys. The German forces built the most outstanding examples under the generic name "Zeppelins" after the aristocratic designer of this type of aerostat. The basic principle was to stretch an envelope filled with hydrogen over a rigid structure made from a light alloy

The history of these Zeppelins, the first of which took flight in 1900, included the first aerial bombardment of Paris in 1916, the first commercial crossing of the Atlantic in 1928, and the Hindenberg fire which took 35 lives in New York in 1937, a tragedy that marked the end of the dirigible saga due to their basic structural defect, the fact that they were inflated with an inflammable gas.

During the 1920s, in the course of war reparations, Germany furnished France with two of its enormous dirigibles, including one that would be rebaptized Dixmude. 266 m long and 28 m high, containing 70,000 m³ of hydrogen gas, the dirigible was transported to the base at Cuers-Pierrefeu, where the construction of immense new hangars for these flying objects had just been completed.

On 21 December 1923, the dirigible, no doubt hit by lightning, caught fire and exploded while in flight off the shore of Sicily. Only the body of its captain, Lieutenant Commander Du Plessis, was recovered from the sea that swallowed the other 49 victims. It was then decided to erect this monument in Corsican granite that now lends an original touch to the village of Pierrefeu-du-Var.

An association, Friends of the Dixmude, perpetuates the memory of this tragedy. You can contact the former president, Monsieur Tissier, always ready to tell this dramatic story.

The French Navy still makes use of the aerodrome near Pierrefeu-du-Var and preserves, carefully packed away in a wooden box, a strikingly realistic model of the Dixmude, 3 m long. It might be a good idea to take it out one day and put it on display …

* The name of Dixmude was given to this dirigible to honour the memory of the Belgian resistance to German occupation. Dixmude is a town in Belgium where a bloody battle took place. The Belgians put up a heroic fight there against German assaults in November 1914. .

OFFICE DE TOURISME DE PIERREFEU-DU-VAR
20, boulevard Henri-Guérin, 83390 Pierrefeu-du-Var • Tel: 04 94 28 27 30
• Fax: 04 94 28 21 78 • E-mail : contact@ot-pierrefeu.com

# EXTRAORDINARY EX-VOTOS

• Sanctuaire Notre-Dame-des-Anges
Frères Franciscains de l'Immaculée, 83790 Pignans
T• el: 04 94 59 00 69 • E-mail: ffindanges@immacolata.com
• The sanctuary is open daily, with daily Mass at 7.00 and on Sunday at
10.30 and 17.00

> *A caiman dedicated to the Virgin Mary*

The Notre-Dame-des-Anges chapel that sits on a peak in the Massif des Maures, 10 km from Pignans, is worth a visit for its extraordinary collection of ex-votos, although unfortunately a number of them have been stolen.

One of them, hanging from the chapel ceiling, is an actual stuffed caiman, said to be a victim of Jules Gérard's rifle (see page 238). But the most moving of these ex-votos is probably the photo that features on the cover of the small booklet by Henry Levert (sold by the monks for €10) and representing the execution of four men by a firing squad of eleven soldiers, with Toulon harbour in the background. It's a pity that someone stole another photo showing a hunter of Pignans whose gun had exploded and found himself surrounded by flames, "while the Infant Jesus, in the arms of his mother, peed on the gun". (Source: *Guide de la Provence mystérieuse*, Éditions Tchou).

Legend has it that Nymphe, the sister of St Maximin and servant of Mary Magdalene, lived here long before the existing chapel was built in the 19th century. She is said to have sculpted the statue of the Virgin that stands there today. It was lost but then found again, hidden away in the bushes. The parishioners of Pignans put it inside their church for safekeeping, but the statue returned of its own accord to the bushes. It was then decided that a pilgrimage should be made each year on the first Sunday of July to Notre-Dame-des-Anges. Since 2001, monks from the order of the Frères Franciscains de l'Immaculée live in keeping with their vows inside the sanctuary. On the narrow road that climbs to the summit there is a sign nailed to a tree that seems appropriate: *la beauté de ces lieux fait oublier les peines de la route* [the beauty of this place makes one forget the difficulties along the way].

### UNUSUAL STREET NAMES

In Pignans, when you pass through the door that leads inside the second set of medieval walls by way of the passage de l'Église, you find yourself confronted with a metaphysical choice: on the right you have rue de l'Église (Church) and on the left, rue de l'Enfer (Hell) ... But as it happens, this *enfer* is derived from the old Provençal word, *infèrs*, meaning residues of olive oil, because there was once an olive press in this street (at No. 10). You'll notice that one of the two pretty ceramic panels, illustrating the road to Paradise on the right and the road to Hell on the left, has been broken, no doubt deliberately. Guess which?

# THE STATUE OF JULES GÉRARD

Place des Écoles (near schools and the boulodrome)
• Birthplace of Jules Gérard (the present-day town hall)
7, place de la Mairie, 83790 Pignans

### *Jules Gérard, lion killer*

On 14 June 1817, there was born in Pignans, a wine-growing village in central Var, a certain Jules Gérard. Having lost both his parents early on, the young man demonstrated his zeal for life by developing his physical capacities. He practised hunting because Pignans, surrounded by woods (including the pines that lend the village their name) was rich in game. Fencing and *chausson* (ancestor of French boxing) gave him a taste for combat. When he was 23, he joined up with the corps of Spahis (North African troops serving in the French Army) and was sent to Algeria.

Jules Gérard would commit himself to exterminating the lions that were decimating flocks in the region of Kabylia and sometimes even attacked men.

With the tacit approval of his superiors, he improved on existing techniques for hunting lions. He established procedures to optimize tracking and approaching the wild beasts and helped perfect the weapons that were available at the time. In the mid-19th century, hunting rifles were still relatively primitive.

He shot his first lion in Kabylia in July 1844, at night and using a double-barrelled gun (of which one barrel didn't work), with a single bullet. The beast was over a metre long and weighed 200 kg. From being just another *roumi* (as foreigners were called, in reference to the previous Roman occupation), Jules Gérard came to be a respected figure among the native people, then, as his list of kills grew longer, he was nicknamed Katel Sioud: master of lions.

News of the exploits of the "lion killer" crossed the Mediterranean and became a topic of conversation around dinner tables in Paris. In 1853, Jules Gérard was presented to Emperor Napoleon III. Alphonse Daudet read works by Jules Gérard and was inspired by them to write Tartarin de Tarascon in 1872. But the ridiculous, swaggering character in this book had little in common with the real Jules Gérard.

After killing his 25th lion, Jules Gérard devoted himself to exploration and drowned in the River Jong during an expedition in Sierra Leone. He was 46 years old.

In the place des Écoles at Pignans, you can see the bronze fountain by sculptor Olivier Decamps, inaugurated in 1964 to commemorate the centenary of Jules Gérard's death. And near the door of the town hall, which has a medallion with a lion's head and two stone lions on either side, there is a plaque that recalls that this was the birthplace of Jules Gérard: *Officier des Spahis, chasseur de fauves et écrivain cynégétique dit le tueur de lions* [Spahi officer, hunter of wild beasts and writer on the art of hunting, known as the lion killer].

# THE PROVENÇAL ROBIN HOOD

La Grotte de Gaspard
• Rue Pasteur, 83890 Besse-sur-Issole • Tel: 04 94 69 83 69
• Open afternoons, hours vary according to season.

> **"He walked to his death as if it were a feast"**

Gaspard Bouis was born in Besse-sur-Issole on 9 February 1757. It was during a visit to the village by recruiting sergeants that Gaspard, no doubt under the influence of alcohol typically employed by the military in those times, signed up for the French army. The following day, once the effects of the drink had worn off, he realized that he had made a huge mistake. But as he had already signed the contract, either he joined his unit or became an outlaw. He chose the latter course of action and thus entered history.

To protest against the methods of justice applied in this pre-revolutionary period, Gaspard Bouis, nicknamed Gaspard de Besse by the people of Provence, decided to organize a raid to free Joseph Augias, found guilty of fraud with respect to the *gabelle* [salt tax]. Augias would become one of Gaspard's lieutenants, as would Jacques Bouilly, who also escaped during this raid.

The band organized itself and specialized in attacks on stagecoaches. A few anecdotes soon forged the reputation of this bandit: whenever he robbed a tax collector, the highwayman returned the money to those who had been taxed. And if his motto was, "Frighten, but never kill", when one of his men cut off the finger of a lady to steal her ring, Gaspard did not hesitate to shoot him dead with his pistol.

While these adventures were taking place, the French were building up to their Revolution and generally supported this defender of the poor. Gaspard de Besse found refuge everywhere from the authorities and also seemed to be everywhere. There was not an inn, not a ravine, not a cave in the region that had not seen the passage of Gaspard and his band. The man was both brilliant and elegant, pleasing to women, but less so to their cuckolded husbands ... Was he finally denounced out of jealousy? Whatever the case, Gaspard and his two lieutenants were arrested at Valette-du-Var and sentenced to death by the Parlement de Provence. The execution took place in Aix. Elise Malherbe, niece of the French poet, was in the crowd and witnessed this event. "He walked to his death as if it were a feast, replying with graceful salutes to the kisses blown to him by the crowd. He asked to be allowed to wear his town finery for the occasion. I did not want to see any more ..." Gaspard and his two friends were put to death by means of the *roue* [wheel] on 25 October 1781. None of them had reached the age of 30 ...

At the Grotte de Gaspard, an exhibit on the life and times of Gaspard de Besse offers a further insight into his character.

---

OFFICE DE TOURISME DE BESSE-SUR-ISSOLE
1, place Souleyet, 83890 Besse-sur-Issole • Tel/Fax: 04 94 59 66 57
• e-mail : si.besse@wanadoo.fr

---

# THE STATUE OF ST SUMIAN – J.-L. LAMBOT'S BOAT

Musée du Pays Brignolais, Place du Palais des Comtes de Provence
83170 Brignoles • Tel/Fax: 04 94 69 45 18
• Admission: €4, reduced rate (children aged 6–12, students) €2;
children under 6 free • Open Wednesday to Sunday, 1 April to 30
September: 9.00–12.00 and 14.30–18.00 (Sunday 9.00–12.00 and
15.00–18.00). From 1 October to 31 March: 10.00–12.00 and 14.30–
17.00 (Sunday 10.00–12.00 and 15.00–17.00)
• E-mail: contact@museebrignolais.com
• http://www.museebrignolais.com

*A boat
made from
reinforced concrete*

A roughly carved block of stone, the statue of St Sumian has long been an object of fixation for women of Brignoles longing for children. But its long exposure to the elements (it once stood outside the town ramparts) has made it difficult to "read". It represents an androgynous figure whose two hands join together at the navel (*embouligo* in Provençal: in Brignoles the statue is in fact known as the *embouligue*). The custom is to kiss the part of the statue just below the navel in order to stimulate fecundity. This practice was forbidden by the Church, but the constant shower of erotic kisses has eroded the statue to the point that today you can see a cupule (cup-shaped hollow) caused by the mouths of those worshipping this slightly pagan but decidedly Gallic saint …

Joseph-Louis Lambot's reinforced-concrete boat is the other bizarre curiosity in this museum. Born at Montfort-sur-Argens (Var) in 1814, the young Lambot pursued his studies in Paris, he devoted himself to agriculture on his family's estate. Where did he get the idea of "reinforcing" concrete? Nobody knows. But he employed this technique (inserting a steel framework in the cement) to make fruit crates and shelves, and so can be regarded as the true inventor of reinforced concrete. One fine day, he even decided to build a boat using this material. To everyone's surprise, it floated.

If you visit the museum, don't miss its real treasure, the sarcophagus of La Gayole, the oldest known sarcophagus of Gaulish origin and one of the oldest sculpted sarcophagi in the world (2nd century AD).

---

OFFICE DE TOURISME DE BRIGNOLES
Hôtel de Claviers, 10, rue du Palais, 83170 Brignoles • Tel: 04 94 69 27 51
• Fax: 04 94 69 44 08 • e-mail: info@officedetourisme-brignoles.com
• www.officedetourisme-brignoles.com

---

## SIGHTS NEARBY

### LANCERS' HOUSE

Quite close to the museum, the house at 10 rue des Lanciers was once the home of the guards serving the counts of Provence. At the level of the first storey of this building, hook-shaped stones protrude from the façade. When the lancers finished their guard duties, they would come back to this house to rest. Navigating the narrow spiral staircases with halberd was not very easy, so they used to lean their lance on one of these stones when they arrived. Then, from the first-storey windows, they could take hold of the upper half and lay it down flat, resting on two of these stone hooks, safe from any thieves.

## ABBAYE ROYALE DE LA CELLE

- 9, place des Ormeaux, 83170 La Celle
- Visits: enquire at the Information Centre in La Celle
- Tel/Fax: 04 94 59 19 05
- E-mail: la-celle@wanadoo.fr • http://www.la-celle.fr

> *The abbey was once home to some very naughty nuns*

In the 11th century, the monks of Abbaye Saint-Victor in Marseille founded the Abbaye de la Celle, composed of two Benedictine priories, one for the monks and the other for nuns. Two centuries later, Garsende de Sabran, who had just lost her husband, King Alfonso II of Aragon, came to La Celle in order to take the veil and was elected abbess of the convent, which thereby became "royal". She abandoned Aix-en-Provence and public life, reserving her bewitching beauty for God.

But beginning in the 17th century, a certain decline in moral standards set in: although still bound by their vows of chastity, some sisters obtained "exemptions" and the abbey soon came to resemble a bawdy house: its boudoirs and padded leather cells attracted more and more gentlemen and it's said that, come evening, there could be heard more rustling of silk than prayers … As one chronicler reported, "These nuns could only be distinguished by the colour of their skirts and the first name of their lover …

Once brought to light, the scandal caused the convent to be closed. The abbey was sold as national property during the Revolution and turned into a farm before being bought in 1938 by Sylvia Fournier, owner of the island of Porquerolles. Since 1990; the priory belongs to the Conseil Général du Var which is continuing restoration of the monument. You can visit the magnificent ambulatory, the chapter and the cellar. In the garden of the cloister, some ancient mulberry trees have been saved by treatment of their hollow trunks and sap flows within their bark.

The Sainte-Perpétue church, which was one of the convent chapels, shelters the marble sarcophagus of Garsende de Sabran, whose presence in this place is close to being miraculous. For a long time, it was used as a drinking trough for animals in the village square before sold by its purported owner. Several years later, an antique dealer in Draguignan spotted it at an auction and informed the Musée du Louvre, who blocked the sale. The Conseil Général was able to buy back this property, which should never have left the abbey.

### "AS THIN AS THE GOOD LORD OF LA CELLE"

In the church, the 14th-century crucifix represents a Christ of corpse-like thinness. Today visitors are told that a local saying "As thin as the Good Lord of La Celle" is used to speak of a slender person. In fact, the more frequent expression used in the region is even crueller: "As ugly as the Good Lord of La Celle".

## LAC DU GRAND LAOUTIEN

- On the D64 between Gareoult and La Roquebrussanne
- Parking

*"...And the lake turned blood-red"*

**A**n improbable, unexpected, breathtaking and somewhat disturbing spot, the Lac du Grand Laoutien (Provençal for "basin") lies at the bottom of a veritable crater that inevitably brings to mind a volcano or even the impact of a meteorite.

The lake is 130 m across and 43 m deep, with sheer cliffs rising 30 m in places above the water's surface. The water is green and conceals its shadowy secrets. A strange sensation, looking down into this natural curiosity, and a feeling of contentment on leaving it without having fallen in …

In the past, the inhabitants of the two nearest villages, Gareoult and La Roquebrussanne, were convinced that the lake was a dormant volcano. Each year, on the second Sunday in May, the priest of La Roquebrussanne would have to go down to the shore to bless the waters. If he ever refused, it was said that the volcano would awaken within the year. The phenomenon that took place in 1775 did not reassure anyone as to the mysterious nature of the lake. That year, simultaneously with the earthquake that destroyed the city of Lisbon, the lake turned blood-red.

Another curiosity, the animal species living within this lake are very rare and not found in other French lakes, but only in Nordic countries. It's as if they have survived the warming of the local climate, evolving in an underground environment connected to some yet-to-be-explored network. Of the 13 species of hydracarian present, three are normally only found in northern Europe, two in tropical Africa, and one in Morocco and the Banyuls area. Lastly, we should mention the *Limnogeria lougiseta*, for which this lake is the only known habitat in the world.

As for the volcano, experts think that the Grand Laoutien was once an underground cavity whose roof, overloaded with the weight of trees and rocks, suddenly collapsed.

Two aerial views of the site:
http://www.carto.net/verdon/ste_baume/laloube/laoucien_aerien.htm

```
              S V L A S A S A L V S
                L A S A T A S A L
                  S A T R T A S
                    T R E R T
                    R E C E R
C  R  V  X          E C I C E   A N G E L I C A
                    C I H I C
M                   I H I H I                      M
V I                 H I M I H                    C V
I G V               I M X M I                  M E C
G V F E R I H I M X V X D O     M I N I M E
V F E R I H I M X V R V X D     O M I N I M
F E R I H I M X V R C R V X     D O M I N I
V F E R I H I M X V R V X D     O M I N I M
G V F E R I H I M X V X D O     M I N I M E
I G V               S E X E S                  M E C
V I                 T S E S T                    C V
M                   Q T S T Q                      M
                    V Q T Q V
S.  T H O M A E     A V Q.V A  de  A Q V I N O
                    M A V A M
                    S M A M S
                    E S M S E
                    M E S E M
                    P M E M P
                    E P M P E
                  A R E P E R A
                O D A R E R A D O
              O R O D A R A D O R O
◄  -  -  -  -  -    1 5 , 8  c m .  -  -  -  -  ►
                2 9 5   caractères
```

## THE PALINDROME OF NOTRE-DAME-D'INSPIRATION

Notre-Dame-d'Inspiration
• Chemin de la Chapelle, 83136 la Roquebrussanne
**Access from the village** of La Roquebrussanne: take the path to the
chapel that runs west from the centre of the village. Leave your car in the
parking space next to the oratory at the foot of the path. The climb takes
a good quarter of an hour by this route, at first paved with pebbles (and
good intentions), then becomes a dirt track.

The bell of the Notre-Dame-d'Inspiration chapel is unusual in that it has a curious palindrome inscribed on its sides. Brought from Rome in 1730, it was cast by a certain Casini, "caster of the reverend works of St Peter in the Vatican". The palindrome, in the shape of a cross, is composed of 295 characters which were decrypted by Abbé Menin,

> *The 295 characters of the palindrome inscribed upon the bell still preserve their secret*

a former priest, as follows: "The cross is for me certain salvation. It is the cross that I worship always. Angelic cross. The cross of the Lord with me. The cross is for me a refuge, Saint Thomas Aquinas." But that's only the tip of the iceberg. The essential part of the palindrome is obscure, to say the least.

The palindrome is displayed on the visible portion of the bell, but given the height of the belfry, you'll need binoculars or a good telephoto lens to see it. And to actually read it, you'd better bring a ladder …

The Notre-Dame-d'Inspiration chapel is at the top of a hill overlooking the village of La Roquebrussanne, which also features the ruins of a chateau and a beautiful amphitheatre built by a former priest using stones from this chateau. It is almost regrettable that this amphitheatre, capable of seating over a thousand people, has not been put to use by some festival or other, given its splendid location.

**PALINDROMES**

A palindrome is a sentence that can be read in both directions, starting from the right or the left. There are palindromes of letters, syllables, or whole words. Here are some famous examples of palindromes in French: *Tu l'as trop écrasé, César, ce Port-Salut, Un roc cornu, Cerise d'été, je te désire.* (to be read in a circle, with the "C" in the middle), *Non à ce canon !, Karine égarée rage en Irak, Oh, cela te perd répéta l'écho …*
The longest palindrome in French literature is that of Georges Pérec: "Le Grand Palindrome" (1969), included in *La Littérature potentielle*, Collection Idées, Gallimard, 1973.

OFFICE DE TOURISME DE LA ROQUEBRUSSANNE
15, avenue Georges-Clemenceau, 83136 La Roquebrussanne
• Tel: 04 94 86 82 11 • www.la-roquebrussanne.fr

# ALPHABETICAL INDEX

# THEMATIC INDEX

## BARS, RESTAURANTS, HOTELS AND SHOPS

## CHILDREN

## CURIOSITIES

## GARDENS AND WALKS

## HISTORY AND PRE-HISTORY

## INDUSTRIAL HERITAGE

## MUSEUMS

## RELIGION AND ESOTERICA

## SCIENCE AND EDUCATION

**Acknowledgments:**
**The author** would like to give special thanks to Suzanne Boudeau for her comments and advice on the text, and also extend thanks to Robert Alberti, Eichi Awoki, Michel Baconnet, Hervé Barelli, Jean-Paul Barelli, Pierre Berenguier, Christian Berkesse, Claude Bernard, Fernand Bertejo, Laurent Boissin, Marc Boriosi, M^me Servera Boutefoy, Pascal Brocchiero, Richard Caireschi, Philippe Cantarel, Simone Chambourlier, Frédérique Citerabullot, Laure Clément, Brigitte Cohen Tanaudji-Dahan, Christian Delseray, Béatrice di Vita, Florent Duchêne, Patrick Elouarghi, Laurent Eplé, M. Falconnet, M. and M^me Farinelli, Éditions Flohic, Serge Fournel, Gaston Franco, Raymond Gay, D^r Jean-Yves Girard, Juliette and Mireille Giraud, Pierre Godlewski, Alain Gumiel, David Hameau, Mauricette Hintzy, Pierre Ipert, D^r Philippe Jellinek, Roland Joffre, M. and M^me Didier Kulacinski, M. Lambert, Frédéric Lanore (extremely generous with his time), Elisabeth Lara, Patrick Le Tiec, Sandrine Legendre, Sandrine Léonard, Nathalie Leydier, David Lisnard, Pierre-Guy Martelli, Thierry Martin, Sylvain Massa, Christophe Messineo, Sandrina Michon, Christine Million, Anne-Lise Mortelmans, the Musée de l'Artillerie, Raymond Négrel, Mado Nésic Perichon, Jean-Marc Nicolaï (extremely generous with his time), Isabelle Nohain, Karine Osmuk, Nadia Ounaïs, Laure Pastore, Patricia Paula, Sandra Philippe, Patrick Piguet, M^me Pugi, M^me Ricord, Philippe Rigollot, Didier Rostagne, Evelyne Runfoca, Bernard Savatier, M^me Servera Boutefoy, David Singleton, Marie-Hélène Squillante, M^me Strazzulla, Didier Théron, Sabrina Tissot, Aline Torlet, Renaud Vassas, Christian Vialle, Alain Vittersheim, Comité départemental du tourisme du Var, Comité régional du tourisme Côte d'Azur, Comité départemental du tourisme du Var, the Comité régional du tourisme Côte d'Azur, the Comité régional du tourisme PACA, the Conseil général du Var, the Conseil général des Alpes-Maritimes, the DRAC PACA along with its librarians and documentalistes, as well as all the municipalities and tourist offices who opened their doors to us.
**The publisher** would like to give thanks to Florence Amiel, Dan Assayag, Émilie de Beaumont, Kees and Aude van Beek, Florent Billioud, Antoine Blachez, Christine Bonneton, Ludovic Bonneton, Louis-Marie Bourgeois, Jean-Baptiste Bourgeois, Philippe Darmayan, Charles Eon, Agnès and Mikael Eon, Vincent Formery, Philippe Gloaguen, Azmina Goulamaly, Romaine Guérin, Antoine Jonglez, Aurélie Jonglez, Stéphanie and Guillaume Jonglez, Timothée Jonglez, Stéphanie Kergall, Ghislain de La Hitte, Hervé du Laurent, Florence and Pierre Merveilleux du Vignaux, Sophie Mestchersky, Marianne and Fabrice Perreau-Saussine, Francois and Sally Picard, Patricia de Pimodan, Valérie Renaud, Stéphanie Rivoal, Pierre Santoul, Damien Seyrieix, Vadim Smith, Henri Villeroy, Raphaëlle and Matthieu Vincent, Karine Zacharias.

**Photo credits:**
All photos by **Jean-Pierre Cassely,** except:
p. 36 © Musée océanographique de Monaco, p. 60 (b. r.) Hi-Hôtel © Patrick Gries and Uwe Spoering, p. 62 © Stéphane Bidault - www.jetons-monnaie.net, p. 130 © Office de tourisme de Cagnes-sur-Mer, p. 172 © Château de Gourdon, p. 198 © Les amis de Saint-Ferréol et du Vieux Lorgues.

P. 42: Le Corbusier, Le Cabanon à Roquebrune -Cap Martin 1952 © F.L.C./Adagp, Paris 2007

**Cartography:** Michelin - autorisation n° 0612400, © Michelin et Cie
**Design:** Roland Deloi - **Layout:** Oriane du Laurent - **Copy-editing/proof-reading (French text):** Marielle Gaudry - **English translation:** Thomas Clegg and Caroline Lawrence

**© JONGLEZ 2007**
Registration of copyright : April 2007 – Edition : 01
ISBN : 978-2-9158-0719-6
Printed in France by Mame - 37000 Tours